"Confessions of a tro

Leslie J. We

For my grandchildren

'If the Almighty plays a musical instrument, surely it is the trombone'
(Attributed to Author George Bernard Shaw)

Copyright © 2015 by Leslie J. Weddell   All Rights reserved

No part of this book may be reproduced, stored in a retrieval system, or transmitted by any means without the written permission of the author.

Dedicated to the memory of Dr. Leslie Kilgren PH.D; also a trombonist, who, during her short life on this Planet, encouraged me to write and enjoy the pleasures of the written word.

1.

'Recruit Weddell'

"Ef 'ight, Ef 'ight, Ef 'ight – GET IN STEP, WEDDELL!!" The voice of our mentor boomed across the parade ground.

Sergeant Crowther was our Drill Instructor, or 'D.I', and a fellow Scot, and didn't like me at all. I was sure of it. Because I was a lanky lad of 6ft.5ins I stood out like a flagpole above the other recruits.

"Squaa-d……HALT!" He roared; the letter 'T' ending as a high pitched squeak.

It was November of 1951, and I had just arrived as a boy recruit at the Royal Marines School of Music, two days prior to this first training Parade.

I was wearing a very itchy, and oversized blue serge uniform along with the thick woollen socks that had been issued to me from the Barracks stores. Inside the huge hobnailed boots, my poor feet hurt like heck because the military footwear of yesteryear was made of stiff new leather, and they had rubbed the skin almost off my heels.

Added to this discomfort, was the fact that we were standing on a parade ground exposed to the elements, on a cold and frosty morning.

Just two days before, I had arrived at the Royal Marines School of Music Barracks in the small Kentish coastal town of Deal, situated between Dover and Sandwich, two of the former five Cinque Ports of Hastings, New Romney, Hythe, Dover, and Sandwich.

Deal has a castle with a long history behind it; known as the most impressive of the 'Device Forts' or 'Henrician' Castles built by King Henry V111 between 1539 and 1540 as an artillery fortress to counter the threat of invasion, brought about by the alliance between Charles V, Holy Roman Emperor and King Francis 1 of France in 1538.

As this is not a history lesson, it is suffice to say that this castle at Deal, along with its neighbouring Castles at Walmer and Sandown, was intended to dominate the Downs, a sheltered area of water in the English Channel protected by the Goodwin Sands, which would have been an ideal rallying point for any invasion fleet.

Phew! End of history lesson. Thought you ought to know though, because apart from that castle there is nothing else that could be called a landmark, in the town.

Just a few days before, I had celebrated my sixteenth birthday at home with my mother in Walsall, an industrial town in the midlands of England. I had told her how much I was looking forward to becoming a Royal Marine Bandsman. As I gazed across the vast expanse of the parade ground of the Royal Marines Barracks, I was wondering what I had got myself into.

My feet hurt, and my heart was thumping like an air hammer as I observed the formidable bulk of Sgt. Crowther, marching rapidly towards me swinging his right arm skywards and pushing his chest out like a prize cockerel.

The polished brass plate on his pacing stick under his left arm gleamed like a diamond in the morning sunlight, and the razor sharp creases in his trousers plus the prominent three gold braided stripes on the upper sleeve of his immaculate deep blue serge tunic, stated his position in life, or more to the point, my life, and that of my fellow recruits, for the next three months.

His hat was precisely in the middle of his shaven head, and his steely eyes missed nothing from beneath the highly polished black plastic peak that glistened like a mirror. I could feel my knees trembling, as he finally stopped abruptly in front of me and bellowed in his thick Glaswegian accent "Weddell! – You long streak of pish - what the hell dae you think yer doin?"

I could hear the other recruits trying to stifle a sniggering laugh.

"Shut up the lot of ye!" he bellowed, still in my face. He had not moved a muscle as his voice ascended to a banshee scream. He couldn't have been more than six inches away from my chin and I could smell his garlic breath. Perhaps he had been for an Italian meal the night before, or had some weird fetish of cooking his eggs with garlic in them. I would never know, but his breath sure did pong.

"You're marching like a bloody pregnant duck! This is no a 'holiday camp! You're here to become a Royal Marine - do you unerstan' me?"

"Yes Sir" I said in a weak and nervous voice that I did not recognize as mine.

I honestly thought he was going to have a seizure, for his face turned a bright purple as he drew himself to his full height and roared "Don't call me Sir! I'm a non commissioned officer and that means you address me as Sergean'. DO YE UNERSTAN?'

People walking their dogs on the seafront, less than half a mile away must have been able to understand. Sergeant Crowther rarely pronounced words correctly that contained the letters 'T' or 'D'

I gulped and blurted out "Sorry Sergeant, I didn't know." I felt like crying at any moment. He walked away to bellow at another unfortunate who had the audacity to speak through the corner of his mouth to the recruit next to him.

The other lads who had arrived a few days before me had already experienced Sgt. Crowther, saying he was a real terror; and under no circumstances should you ever speak to him unless he asked you a question, and even then your life could be made a misery if you did not chose your words carefully.

I had a feeling of dread that our little one-sided tete-a-tete was not entirely over, for the good sergeant started marching briskly back towards me and we were nose to nose once again. The tone of his voice suddenly changed down to a lower gear as he said softly "An' I promise you this Laddie - you will be a Marine by the time I'm finished with ye!"

Sgt. Crowther stepped back one pace and said in a matter of fact manner "Extra parade for this man."

The Corporal that lurked in the background of our DI, was a little man of Welsh decent named Alyn Lloyd, who repeated the instruction in his soft and pleasant accent. "Extra Parade for recruit Weddell". This was, in fact, a punishment parade to remind slack recruits like me, to shape up!

Smiling at me, as he continued "You will enjoy this one, Jock, for it is in the drill shed at 6pm, and it is nice and warm, and you will be wearing a full backpack. Make sure you include everything on the list to go into your pack, and the clothing and equipment is clean and ironed, for you will be laying it out on your service issue blanket on the drill shed floor for inspection. I advise you not to be late, or you will make the NCO in charge very cross."

He walked away a couple of paces, writing something in his notepad, then casually walked back to me with another big smile on his face as he announced with some degree of satisfaction "Sorry Jock, didn't I mention it? Sergeant Crowther will be taking the extra parade tonight."

My heart sank. Not because the dreaded Sgt. Crowther was taking the parade.

That was worrying enough, but what really hit home was the fact that 6pm was Dinner time and it finished at 6.30, which meant I would get no food until breakfast the next morning. Since we were new recruits, we were not allowed to leave the barracks and go 'outside' to the fish and chip shop on the road close to the East Gate of our barracks. We could smell that delicious aroma in our barrack room quarters, up to eleven o'clock every night except Sundays, and it used to drive us mad with hunger. And in those days, there was no such thing as 'Home delivery'!

There was no NAAFI (canteen/shop for servicemen) back in those days in the East barracks, so the dining rooms, or mess, was the only source of food for us green horns. They fed us well, for teenagers can consume large quantities, and the chefs were not stingy with portions because they knew we would burn off the calories with the active life we engaged in daily. We ran everywhere, as opposed to marching, unless it was a lesson in precision parade marching.

We had PE (Physical Exercise) daily for half an hour either in the warmth of the gymnasium in winter, or outside on the grass in nice weather, and if that was not enough, we would do squad runs wearing full back packs every month or so for anything from five to ten miles, depending on who was taking us.

As anyone that has served in the armed forces of their country can tell you, basic training is designed to harden recruits, and turn them into fighting men and women, who will respond instantly to orders from Officers.

The NCO in charge, of course, was on a bicycle for these runs, and any recruit that turned out to be a weakling and could not keep up, was given a revision course, and if he (or she) failed that, they were discharged as unsuitable from the Corps.

As the weeks rolled by and we became fit, smartly turned out recruits, our marching improved, and as we learned to become more expert in playing our chosen instrument, we were allocated to either Parade Band A or B. A Band was the premier one, of course, and the best players would be allocated to it, and the rest of us in Band B, would be inspired to 'get good enough' to be selected for the A Band.

We all were encouraged to play sports to fight obesity, and there was not much of that in my squad. In fact, I don't recall anyone being overweight at all in those early years. And of course we marched up and down that huge parade ground playing music for the other recruits, those that were riflemen and in training, that eventually would become Royal Marine Commandos.

This life as a Marine did not seem anything like the vision I had seen of the Massed Bands of the Royal Marines performing at the Royal Tournament in the Earls' Court Exhibition Centre in London.

They were smartly dressed and played marvellous music. I knew straight away that I wanted to join the Royal Marines Band and become a musician, just like those men I had seen on that day when we were taken there by Mr. Rask, the Bandmaster at my old boarding school.

My mother had agreed to let me join the Royal Marines Band Service as a boy, and I was accepted, and as I say, sent to the boys wing of the school of Music situated in Deal. I would continue with my school education, as well as be trained as a Junior musician until my eighteenth birthday. Then I would be transferred over to the men's barracks and start my service life for real, in the Royal Marines Band Service.

At last, the parade was over. We had finally been dismissed from the cold of the parade ground and returned to the warmth of our dormitories. There was much laughter at my encounter with Drill Instructor Crowther, and Charlie Tomkinson, who billeted in the bed next to mine, said "Well you sure made a pal today!"

"Aye Jock, ye sure did!" and lots of exaggerated 'Ochs' and other guttural sounds came forth from the many mimics trying to do a Scottish accent.

"Take no notice of this lot Leslie, for they are no better than you or me." The comforting words came from fellow recruit Cyril Beamish, who had been appointed our room lance Corporal.

The name Cyril took me right back to my childhood, and the wonderful days with my little brother, living on a Scottish Farm.

2.

Dodridge Farm, Midlothian, Scotland. 1940

On any other night at 9.30pm, in the tranquil surroundings of Dodridge Farm in the Scottish County of Midlothian, we would all be tucked up in our beds fast asleep. But on this particular night, my little brother Cyril and I had been rudely awakened by a deep and ominous droning sound.

It was August of 1940 and I was nearly 6, but I took hold of my four year old brother's right hand and we shuffled through the kitchen in our pyjamas, turned the latch key on the back door, and stood in our bare feet on the back steps of our cottage, sleepily staring up at the clear night sky.

Of course I cannot remember doing this, but the story was told to me by my sister, Jeanette, known to us all in the family as Nettie, when I was old enough to understand, for she had been looking out her bedroom window trying to see what was making the droning noise in the sky.

There was a gap between the back door of the cottage and the outhouses that held the laundry room, and to the right of that there was the outdoor toilet, plus a coal house and a small tool shed. We stood there on those stone steps, gawping up through the gap between the building. A carpet of stars spread across the heavens, and the air was sweet with the scent of newly cut wheat standing in rows of stacks, or 'stookies' as we called them, in the fields surrounding the farm buildings and cottages.

Then we discovered the source of the rumbling sound, for the sky was full of aircraft approaching Dodridge Farm from the South East, and we stared in awe at the planes as they came ever closer.

They were Luftwaffe (German) Air Force Heinkel He 111 Bombers; and the Civil Defence searchlights had trapped a small group of them in a bright crisscross of piercing light, as the planes weaved their way through the sky towards Edinburgh and Glasgow docks.

The anti aircraft, or 'ack-ack' guns as they were nicknamed by the public, opened fire from the defence artillery installations situated at strategic points around the Scottish countryside. We could see the results of their futile efforts as the shells exploded harmlessly in mid air, completely missing the aircraft as they continued relentlessly on their way to deliver their cargo of death and destruction.

The Nation did not know it at that time, but the Luftwaffe bombing raids on the major ports of Scotland and England were just a tiny part of the Chief of the German Air Force Air Marshall Goering's plan to starve and demoralise the British nation, by destroying the urgently needed food and supply ships arriving from the United States and Canada, that had managed to escape the U-boat attacks in the Atlantic Ocean.

Glasgow and Edinburgh were not the only docks to get a devastating hammering; London, Liverpool, Manchester, Hull, Bristol, Cardiff, Portsmouth and Plymouth also got the full treatment. In addition to this, munitions and weapon manufacturing factories in the cities of Coventry and Birmingham, Glasgow, Cardiff, and Newcastle, were heavily bombed night and day immediately the initial air raids had started in London.

Goering was paving the way for his master, Adolf Hitler, to implement his grand plan to break the British Nation's spirit before his storm troopers strutted into England and spread the black swastika over the whole nation, to seal the final stage of the Nazi domination of Europe.

Cyril and I thought it was exciting to watch those planes droning overhead, and at such a tender age we had no idea they were the enemy; and had no comprehension of the pain and loss of life that was about to happen within the hour, when those aircraft unloaded their deadly cargo of incendiary bombs on the docks, and surrounding workers' homes.

According to my sister, who related all this to me in later years, there must have been over two hundred bombers. As they came ever closer to our cottage, the noise of the engines became deafening, and as we stood with our mouths open looking up at the planes, we suddenly felt Dad's big hands grabbing the tops of our Pyjamas.

"Get inside!" he roared "What on earth do you think you are playing at? The kitchen door is wide open - do you want them to drop a bomb on us?" The fact that we had no lights on in the house made no difference to our Dad!

"Silly little monkeys!" Dad shouted.

We began to cry, and our little hearts sank further as Mum suddenly appeared from out of her bedroom. She had lit a candle instead of switching on the electric light, and there was a remarkable resemblance in her shadowy appearance to that of a lady from the Victorian era, for she was wearing a long white nightgown and floppy nightcap, comically stretched askew over her old fashioned metal hair curlers.

She looked at us sternly, and at Dad with a quizzical expression, as she inquired, "What on earth is going on?"

Father told her.

She hissed softly at us "Get to bed now; I'll deal with you two in the morning!"

Happily for us, she had forgotten all about the incident by breakfast time.

In those days we kids did as our Parents told us, without question. It was not that they were unkind. On the contrary, they were both caring and loving parents.

They were strict, in the same manner their own parents had been in bringing them up. They just wanted to do the right thing, and teach us to avoid the mistakes they had made when they were young.

Electricity on the Farm was restricted to the Farmer's house and the cow sheds, where it was required for the milking equipment and lighting the sheds; and when needed in severe winter weather to heat the sheds for the animals.

It did not arrive in the cottages until 1944, when the farmer had a stroke of luck and got a government grant to install electricity to all his tenant properties, and also erect two street lights on the short strip of tarmac road leading up from the farm to the six cottages.

On reflection, I now know it did me a lot of good to respect my folks and other elders, for it taught me values seemingly lost to so many of the youngsters of today.

My father, John Weddell, was a taciturn man most of the time and good natured to everyone including his family. I never ever heard him use bad language, and he was polite and respectful to others at all times. But like any other father, if either of us boys went over the top being silly, he would be firm and start to unbuckle his thick leather waist belt to administer retribution, if need be.

Thinking about it, both my parents must have had the patience of Job with me; for as we grew up I became more boisterous, and although Cyril was a relatively quiet lad, I was, to be frank, a real pain in the butt. In today's terms, an apt description of my behaviour in those days would be a 'Dennis the Menace' type boy, for I always seemed to be up to some mischief.

Rightly so, I was punished a couple of times when I deserved it, with Mum trying to intervene by placing herself protectively in front of me, shouting to my Dad "Don't you hit him!" but her pleas were not always successful, and I would feel a tinge of pain from that leather belt as it made contact with my backside.

I recall such an occasion when I felt the width of that belt.

It was mid summer time and there had been no rain for weeks. With my friends, the other children on the farm, I decided to show them I was a boy of action, and decided to use a box of 'Swan Vestas' matches and play a silly game.

This involved a haystack that was a good 20 feet tall and perhaps 100 feet in diameter, and dry as tinder. This would be in a silo these days, but back then it was simply in the open air, with a tarpaulin at best, to cover it and keep out the rain. I don't know exactly how old I was, but my sister related this story to me later in life too, and reckons I would be perhaps nine years old.

The very fact that I had taken the matches from the top of the mantle piece above the cooking range in our home, also added to my thoughtless crime. It was a silly game, but at the time, I and the other kids must have thought it was a thrill to pull out a strand of hay and light it up, pinching it out before it got to the rest of the hay behind it. We got away with it several times, but trouble was destined to happen, and it did.

Instantly, the whole Hay Stack went up in flames and all the kids ran away, telling their Parents who had 'done it'. I was thrashed by that belt of Dad's and taken to the Farmer and had to apologise, and promise never to do anything as stupid ever again. Even back then, that was a valuable gathering of hay, for it was stored to feed the animals in the sheds during the cold months of winter.

It never crossed my mind at that age that my Father could have been sacked from his job and all of us kicked out of the cottage and asked to leave the farm for good.

That talking to by the farmer must have been like water off a duck's back, for several months later I was back in trouble again. If nothing else, we kids knew how to invent games to keep ourselves amused!

No video or internet games or music players, mobile phones, or anything else the youth of today keeps itself amused with. We had to employ our own ways of amusement.

One hot summer day we decided to play a 'dare' game, and yours truly came up with the 'brilliant idea' of pushing my head in between the cross bars of a wooden gate, only to get it firmly lodged.

Of course, all the kids were roaring with laughter, me included. It was only when I began to panic that little Cyril took the initiative to go and get help. He brought back Mum, carrying a half pound of precious lard, which she used to grease my neck and sides of my head, but to no avail, because I was stuck fast. Other Mother's tried to help free me too, suggesting this and that way, but to no avail.

You can imagine the look on the Farmers face when he had to drop everything he was doing, to bring a saw and cut the gate spar so I could be freed. He was not amused, and took the cost of replacing the sturdy wood spar out of my father's wages for that week.

In return, I felt the wrath of my dad and his leather belt and was grounded for a fortnight with no pocket money. It certainly taught me a lesson not to show off in front of the other kids, without first thinking of the consequences.

It was only later in life that (again thanks to my sister) I was told that the Farmer was really a very nice man, and understanding. He thought I was a tearaway, but basically a good kid, and he really valued my Dad's skills and work input at Dodridge Farm. That was the real reason he did not dismiss my Father from his job, or ask us to leave our cottage home.

Although he had served as a Cavalryman in the Royal Artillery in WW1, my Father was not selected for service in 1940 because he was considered too old at fifty one. He was graded as an essential farm worker, and was one of only three men allowed to stay and work with the owner of Dodridge farm; one of hundreds of Scottish farms that supplied milk, eggs, grain, and meats, to the national food chain.

Even now, after all those years have passed by, I still have a vision of my Father sitting in his favourite chair wearing his clean working clothes of collarless shirt and brown corduroy breeches, all held together by the aforementioned thick leather belt with that huge brass buckle securing it all to his wiry frame.

Every evening he would walk wearily into the back porch after a hard day's work, and unlacing his hobnailed working boots, he would place them near the back door ready for the following morning.

In those days, there were no proper bathrooms in our farm workers cottages, so the whole family had to wash in the laundry room.

This was quite roomy and warm enough when the boiler fire had been lit beneath the large copper pot filled with water, that served for boiling the clothes, as well as our means of cleansing ourselves once it had been cleaned out for the purpose.

Bath time for us kids was fun! I remember a white enamel bucket being used to pour the clean, warm water over our heads as we both sat in that man-sized tin bath tub, and then with Mum supervising us whilst we soaped up, and scrubbed ourselves, laughing and messing around, as kids will.

We would then get the final deluge of clean water from the second enamel bucket over our heads, and being wrapped in a large fluffy towel, we would be quickly transferred from the laundry room into the house, and in no time at all, be standing on the carpet in front of the coal fire in the front room, in our birthday suits!

'Cuticura' talcum powder was then liberally sprinkled over us both, and then it was on with the pyjamas and placing our little hands around a small cup of warm milk, after which, it was off to bed.

On his return to the cottage and after shedding his boots, Dad would usually enter the laundry room, and stripping off, he would pick up the hard slab of red carbolic soap (the only soap I can remember from those days) and follow the same ablution system as we did, with the buckets.

This routine went like clockwork every day, with my mother fetching bucket after bucket of water from the kitchen sink tap in the house, and pouring it into the copper boiler and lighting the wood stove beneath it an hour before Dad was due home.

Being a thrifty housewife, she knew just the right amount of water to use, for heating that copper required firewood, and to get it meant a weekly trip to the nearby woods for my Dad and the other Dads in the cottages, to gather enough small logs to last seven days. Coal was only used for the house grate fire for cooking and heating water, which also supplied an antiquated radiator system that my Dad and Uncle George (when he visited us once in a while, for he was in the army) would clean out the clogged up system in summer.

The advantages of living in the countryside during wartime are many, and we were very lucky that there were plenty of trees on the farm. We were allowed to chop up those that had fallen, and since there were only six cottages and the Farmer's house, there was always plenty of firewood to go around.

Clean clothes were neatly laid out for Father, and he would then enter the house and sit down at the kitchen table and enjoy his evening meal.

After some light conversation with all of us, he would walk through into the small front room and sit in his favourite chair, besides the old fashioned brown lacquered wooden framed Pye radio on a table, which also contained a large mug of tea, his 'Woodbine' cigarettes and matches, and a folded newspaper.

The radio had a see-through glass accumulator battery which supplied the electrical current, which 'the man in the mobile shop van' would take back every fortnight and replace with a freshly charged one, and Dad would listen to the BBC six o'clock news. Lighting up a cigarette, he would then read his copy of 'The Scotsman' newspaper.

He followed this same routine day in, and day out. The only time he strayed from it was when he would put on his best suit (always having to be hung in the washroom that afternoon by our elder sister, for a couple of hours to rid it of the overpowering pong of mothballs!) to take our mother to a dance in the nearest village of Pathead, three miles away, on the last Saturday night of each month.

There was a bus service, but you had to walk about a quarter of a mile down a hill to the main road to catch it. Country folk don't mind this at all, as they are used to walking everywhere. Many a time, my Parents missed the last bus home and walked the three miles from the village back to the Farm. Dad enjoyed those nights out, but although I don't recall him ever complaining, I bet he was not too thrilled about having to get up at 4 am on Sunday mornings to go into the barns to help feed the livestock, and milk the dairy herd.

Most folks did not have much money back then, and taking a taxi home from the dance was out of the question. To Mum and Dad, that was better spent on buying fish and chips, but often by the time they got home the food would be stone cold.

Didn't matter too much because it was Saturday night, and Cyril and I were allowed to get out of bed and go eat some of the fish and chips after Mum had warmed them up again in the kitchen oven, which was usually still hot, as the fire was never allowed to completely die out.

From our back garden, we could see a patchwork of fields either lying fallow or filled with vegetables, corn, wheat, barley, or animals out to graze, with the boundary hedgerows stretching away into the distance on all sides.

It's strange how I can remember some things vividly from early childhood, yet other images and information just will not appear.

But there is one strong memory I still have, and that is about the urgent need to use the outside toilet during winter! Visiting that drafty little room with the wind blowing in the gap under the door as you sat there shivering, was not for those who were faint of heart. It was sparsely decorated with whitewashed walls and one homemade toilet roll holder, which contained cut up newspapers, as we could not afford toilet rolls, although there was a brand named 'Bronco' available, but most working families used cut up newspapers instead. We did not realize the danger of the print on those sheets, but no my knowledge, it did not make any of us ill in any way.

You had to take a 'hurricane' kerosene lamp with you, as there was no electric light until 1944. The lamp was placed on a nail, my Father had hammered into one of the two wooden beams that held the water cistern up, and when it was windy, the lamp would sway, casting weird looking shadows on the walls around the little room, and it goes without saying, that nobody in our family spent more time in there than they really had to.

When a heavy snowfall came down, my Dad would have to keep a shovel in the kitchen so he could eventually get the back door open, by having sometimes to climb out a window, to clear the snow away from the doors then clear a path to the toilet, and the coal shed, plus the laundry area.

Why the architect and builders never actually put the most important facility in the warmth of the house or at least, the laundry building, I will never know. This was of course many years before all homes in Britain eventually got inside bathrooms fitted, which did not come until the 1950's or later, for most people.

One of the pleasures of growing old is to have good memories, and I still can see that beautiful Scottish landscape in my mind as clear as it was back in the 1940's.

The colour contrasts of trees, bushes and fields, as the seasons came and went; from the bright multi colours of Autumn on the trees about to shed their leaves, to the fairyland appearance of the landscape when deep snow drifts covered everything in midwinter, to the joys of Spring and the blooms on trees, the flowers on the hedgerows; the birds singing in the trees and bushes, and the gradual change to the golden hue of the grain crops growing in summer, right up to harvest time.

Millions of children around a war torn World never got to enjoy the most important years of their lives; the joy of having a happy childhood. A time that should be fun packed and full of contentment. Years that I firmly believe, establish character and help to mould a child into a stable, and useful, adult.

I am eternally grateful that I had the opportunity to grow up as a child on a farm in those far off days, and they most certainly were the wonder years for me.

On the occasions when Mum and Dad decided to go for a night out, we were left in the care of our 22 year old sister, Jeannette, who used to boss us about, as big sister's will.

But we did manage to dodge around her most of the time by playing out with the other kids whilst she was with her boyfriend 'snogging' on the sofa in the front room! We used this as ammunition when she started to boss us, for we would 'tell mum and dad' if she did not buy us an ice cream when the van came up the little road to the cottages two nights of the week in the summer months.

Cyril and I knew when we had pushed Dad too far with our constant messing about and wrestling around on the floor, for when we saw him put down his paper and start to unbuckle his belt, we were off like a pair of hares and out the door for a couple of hours, until we thought it safe to return and sneak into the kitchen. Mum knew the score, since we always got a cuddle from her and a glass of milk, and maybe a scone or home made biscuit, before the mandatory bath time, followed by the 'Cuticura' treatment, and bed.

Dad used to keep several packets of his favourite 'Woodbines' cigarettes on the high mantelpiece behind the graceful looking curved wooden clock that sat in front of an ornate mirror. It had a glass cover that opened with a little clasp, and he would wind the mechanism and then adjust the time to the six o'clock 'pips' given just before the news, on the radio every evening.

One day late in July when the Adults were all working the harvest in the fields, taking advantage of the long hours of daylight, Cyril and I, who should have been doing our school homework, decided we had to try these things called cigarettes, that Dad loved so much.

Being the tallest, I stood on a chair and reached up with my hand towards the clock on the mantelpiece over the fireplace, all the time with Cyril standing back and giving me directions. I found a new packet of the magical woodbines cigarettes, and brought them down for inspection. They looked harmless enough in the packaging, and we carefully broke open the cellophane covering and removed the silver paper inside.

Hearts pumping, we knew we were doing something we should not have been doing, and being boys, we loved it! We took only one cigarette out of the packet and prepared to light it up. It looked easy, because we had seen our Dad smoking many times, and surely it could not be that hard. We both were wondering what the sensation was like; would it be tasty? Nice aroma? Surely it must be one or both of these things, because Dad seemed to enjoy it.

Finding a box of matches on the shelf, I decided as the oldest brother, that I should go first, and between mucking about and laughing our heads off, I finally managed to get the cigarette lit, and having watched my dad, I took an almighty drag on it. I started to choke, and went into a fit of coughing, and my head began to spin.

Catching my reflection in the mirror, I could see that my face had turned a kind of puce colour. It was horrible. I had never experienced a sensation like that before, and suddenly felt violently sick. I handed the cigarette to Cyril as I fled through the back door and threw up on the garden, next to the rain barrel.

After what seemed an eternity of wrenching my guts out, I turned to go back into the house and see what Cyril was doing, but he was standing right next to me and asking if I was alright. I had not heard him in my misery of vomiting. He still held the burning cigarette in his hand, and grabbing it, I asked if he had tried it and got a firm 'no' in reply. I threw the offending weed on the ground and pushed it with my foot, deep into the soil of the potato plot.

In disgust, I said "Urgh! How can dad enjoy those horrible things?"

When I felt a little better, we went inside the Cottage and made sure the woodbines were put back exactly in the place I had found them. The next day Dad reached up on the Mantelpiece for a new pack of cigarettes. Opening the packet, he shouted "Jeanette, have you been at my ciggies?" Our sister felt hurt, but replied truthfully that she had not. Dad called out to Mum in the kitchen. "Jean, have you had one of my Woodbines?" Again, there was a negative reply. Dad looked stumped for an answer to the mystery, and left it at that.

Even as a child, I could not tell a lie. I felt guilty as hell, and the next day I blurted it out to my Mum. She looked at us both and said "Your Dad would go mad if he found out. Don't you boys smoke a cigarette EVER again." She was wonderful, because she kept our little secret.

3. 'Boy Musician, to instant Adult Musician..'

Back in the Royal Marines barracks in Deal, after a fortnight or so of learning very quickly to keep out of trouble, and trying to be smart and attentive on parade, I had less contact with DI Crowther, who seemed to be satisfied that I was at last, shaping up into some resemblance of what he wanted me to become.

When the morning parade finished, we had a half hour to prepare ourselves to attend school lessons until midday, then we went for lunch. At 1.30pm we reported to our music teachers, who spent the next three hours teaching us to play an instrument, and to read music.

It was on the first visit to music lessons that I was asked what instrument I would like to play. I told the instructor that I played the Brass Bass at school, and asked if it would be alright for me to continue with this instrument.

"Certainly not." The music instructor exclaimed, and promptly produced a trombone. "I want you to learn to play this. We are short of trombone players in the Band Service." So much for the 'what would you like to play' system.

That was it. I had no choice but to accept his 'offer,' and reluctantly began to learn to get a few notes out of the thing, and as the weeks rolled by, I started to produce some decent sounds and it got noticed one day when I was sent for my first lesson with a Bandmaster.

To my everlasting shame I cannot remember his name now so many years later, but he sure could play the trombone and was different from the other instructors, who tended to shout a lot and not pay too much attention to their fledgling charges.

He taught me how to play scales and to read music, and how to produce a good sound, and increase my technique. In about six months, I had made enough progress to be included in the coveted 'Boys 'B' band' and that was a revelation to me, for they were far superior in musicianship than anyone in my old school band.

For the next two years I never missed a music lesson with that wonderful teacher and attended every band practice. Eventually I made it into the 'A' Boy's band, and when the day of my eighteenth birthday had arrived at last, I was marched in double time by none other than Sgt. Crowther, into the Commanding Officer's room.

Before we entered the office, he poked me gently in the chest. His face was kind, and he spoke in a friendly way. I had never seen this side of his character before.

"Well done, Weddell; you've come a long way, and I knew you would turn out for the better. Don't spoil your future by being a buffoon all the time. Your career as a Royal Marine starts now. Right, in you go Laddie! 'ef 'ight, 'ef 'ight…."

Deal Barracks had become known over its long history as the Royal Marine School of Music; the barracks at Walmer consisting of the North, East and South (or Cavalry) barracks, were constructed shortly after the outbreak of the French revolution. Part of the South barracks was used from 1815 as the quarters for the 'blockade men', drafted against a threat of local smuggling. The South barracks became a coastguard station thereafter, and this duty continued until 1840.

It was the East barracks which accommodated the School of Music, until the Royal Naval School of Music was formed at Plymouth in 1903, but which moved to Deal in 1930, replacing the original depot band formed in 1891. Thus the institution became known as the Royal Marine School of Music in 1950. However, in 1996 it was decided that the Royal Marines School of Music be moved to their new quarters in Portsmouth, where they are now based.

So back in the 1950's, it was the East Barracks in which they placed the boys, having moved the Adult males over to new buildings near to the South Barracks. The buildings were very old, and in winter time it was always cold in the rooms, despite ancient looking radiators working. Windows were small, and in summer time the temperature inside those rooms was the complete opposite of winter, for we found it stifling when turning in at night. We had our own cook house and practice rooms, a school, and recreation hall too. The only times we were allowed to go over to the 'men's barracks was when we had to visit the doctor or the dentist.

Over thirty years later a terrible event happened, when at approximately 8:20 am on 22 September 1989, the Royal Marines School of Music was bombed by the IRA (Irish Republican Army) resulting in the deaths of 11 bandsmen, and injuries to 22 other marines. The memorial garden is situated in the grounds of the old barracks where the bomb went off. The memorial garden was built in remembrance of the 11 that died, and was then restored after an arson attack a number of years ago. Every year the families and friends of those that died, join together at the garden to pay their respects and lay flowers in a memorial service.

On the evening of 26 March 1996, the Deal populace were privy to a special ceremony, the Beating Retreat, coming from the South barracks, as the Royal Marines Band Service were commanded to vacate their ancient Kent depot and move to new quarters at Portsmouth. The Royal Marines Band visits Deal every year to the bandstand and puts on a display which attracts over 10,000 people.

Because we were all under the age of eighteen, schooling was compulsory, and we attended five days of the week in the mornings. One of my favourite classes was religious education, for the Depot Naval Padre would take us. He looked a little like Pavarotti, the great Italian singer, for he had the same sort of build, with a large well groomed, but slightly nicotine stained black beard, and would pace up and down the area in the front of the class, chain smoking 'Passing Clouds' cigarettes.

The room was small, and with around twenty of us boys crammed into it, breathing was not easy! I don't know about 'passing clouds,' because our room was full of 'static clouds' of smoke! But he told the most marvelous bible stories, gesticulating with his arms as if he was conducting a symphony orchestra, as he walked from side to side in front of his class with the floor boards creaking under his weight.

He had a marvellous speaking voice that boomed out as he told his stories from memory. No bible was open in front of this man because he knew it from memory, and he held us all spellbound in the half hour or so of the lesson. We would often chuckle to ourselves when we saw him produce a fresh cigarette from somewhere beneath his huge black clerical gown, and watch it disappear into the depths of his thick beard, leaving only a small portion exposed to which he applied the butt of the old cigarette to light it. We were all sure that the beard would one day ignite in the delicate process of re-lighting the new with the old, but it never did happen.

Another treat, was the cooking class. That's what they called it in those days; not 'domestic science' or 'home management' or whatever it is called today. It was one big laugh for a bunch of young teenage lads like us to have a pretty lady teaching us for a change, for all the other teachers were men. She was not your well built jolly cook lady, but a good looking young lass, and I would guess she was in her late twenties. She took no nonsense from anyone, and was most efficient in teaching us to bake scones and simple cakes, as well as basic meals. Secretly we all fell in love with her, of course, because she reminded us of our Mums or sisters back home.

My first posting as an Adult musician, was to the Royal Marines Band stationed in HMS Drake, which was a land based establishment in Devonport, in southern England. All Royal Navy establishments around the World were given names of ships or Admirals or even mythical beasts, such as HMS Drake, HMS Condor, HMS Daedalus, HMS Tamar, or HMS Terror, for example.

It was only a small band of twenty players, but after being there for a few days I realized the reason why; for we did little more than morning parades and occasional Officer's Mess dinners when we were required to play quiet music.
That was a laugh in itself for we were ensconced way up in an old fashioned gallery at the top of the dining room and every little sound went resonating round the mahogany walls with their sombre looking paintings of famous Admirals and naval ships of yesteryear. As soon as we started playing what we thought was quiet music a little door would open behind us and an Officer's mess steward would ask us to 'keep it down a bit'.
As the dinner went down along with the alcohol and the evening wore on, the former civilized conversation between Her Majesty's Royal Navy Officers below us became a babble of noise.
Up would come the same guy again asking if we could play a 'bit louder' as they could not hear us! Happily we obliged, for sitting there in that hot and confined space all squashed up close to each other was no joke and we needed to do something constructive to take our minds off the heat.
So we would play something lively, such as the 'Post Horn Gallop' for that was always a favourite in the mess and they cheered and banged the tables for more at

the end of the tune. This show of appreciation would be measured further by the sudden appearance of a crate of beer for the band, which was always welcome in that hot little space.

Since I had been 'promoted' from a boy musician to Adult musician, the Marines were actually paying me money! It was not much, for if I remember correctly it was around 15 or 16 shillings a week, increasing as I got older.

However, this gave me the chance to buy my very own trombone. I was walking past Moons the music shop in Plymouth town centre, and spotted a shiny new Selmer 'Invicta' model Silver finish trombone hanging in the window.

On inquiring within, it was £29.10.6p, which was a fortune for the likes of me at that time, but the Manager agreed to let me pay weekly for it as I was in uniform at the time I entered the shop.

Of course it was on 'H.P' (Hire Purchase; we call it credit today) When I took it out of the case for the first time in the band room and started to play it, the lads all gathered round to see my new 'toy' for the small bore trombone I had been issued by the Band instruments store back in Deal, was rubbish.

It had been damaged and repaired so many times, loaned out to boy musicians like me and the sound it produced was small and thin in contrast to my nice new trombone.

Being the new kid on the block I was taken under the wing of one of the older guys, who took me into the nearest pub and introduced me to Cider. If you are a Cider drinker, you will have much respect for this potent brew, something I did not have at that time in my youth, as it tasted sweet, and entirely of apples, and was very easily consumed, as if it was a soft drink to quench one's thirst.

It was after a few pints of this agreeable stuff that I realized I had to visit the latrine, and standing up, the room started to spin around and that was the last I remember until I woke up on my bed back in the band quarters.

My 'good friend' that had introduced me to Cider had not even mentioned the alcoholic strength, or the need to drink it slowly and with respect. He had thought the whole 'initiation' ceremony for a rookie was hilarious, and simply phoned the band room and asked two other lads to come down to the pub across the road from the barracks and help him carry me back, sneaking into the camp through a breach in the wire fence, something that could not possibly happen with all the security these days.

From that day onwards I have never touched Cider again. That dreadful experience made me ill for a good 24 hours, and I had to miss a morning parade because of it. The Bandmaster was very cross with me for being so gullible, but he was a good chap and probably saw the funny side of it and left me alone until I had fully recovered.

The weather in Britain in those far off days was pretty much predictable, unlike today with all the global warming changes and advanced weather predicting satellite stations orbiting the Earth. In summer in the UK it was hot, very hot; and in winter time it was freezing. We had lots of snow and ice, yet the population still managed to get to work and keep appointments and children still attended school.

That included us, for the Band was required every morning to march from the Band Room up a long hill incline to reach the parade ground, to perform the morning ceremony of 'colours', which meant a guard of honour of sailors and officers and ourselves, all standing in the freezing cold, in front of a flag pole.

At exactly 8am, they would fire the miniature cannon, which was loaded with a blank, that stood to the right of the base of the flag mast. Note it is a mast, and not a flag pole, in the Navy. The sailors would come to attention and we would play the National Anthem, as the flag was ceremoniously raised up the mast to the top, to flutter in the breeze if there was one, or just hang limp against the mast top.

Then the officer in charge would dismiss us all as quickly as he could, so we could all get back inside a warm building. It was one of these cold mornings that tragedy was to happen; for as we gingerly marched up the hill over the icy surface of the road, we heard a dreadful scream. A workman had fallen off the scaffold around the new petty officer's block being built.

He died on impact, and later we found out he had slipped off an icy portion on the planking on the scaffold that the workers used to access the build. In those days they did not have the all weather covering over the scaffolding, or the strict safety harness regulations in use, today. That dreadful incident was the topic of everyone in the establishment for the next few days.

After 18 months serving in that band, I was posted to another band in HMS 'Condor' a naval training centre for communications, in Arbroath, Scotland. This was right up my street, for I was back in 'God's Country' amongst my fellow countrymen, that could understand my accent!

At that time HMS 'Condor' was full of young Naval apprentices learning the modern communication systems in use on warships, as well as keeping some of the traditional ceremonies going, such as using metaphor flag signalling.

On special occasions such as open days to the public, they would have a display team of young men climbing the rigging of a replica mast head of a sailing ship, and they would spread out along the beams, or yard arms, and go through a well rehearsed routine of signalling with different coloured flags.

It was quite a spectacle, and I doubt if the health and safety act of today would ever allow this to continue. In the 18 month tour of duty there we never had one accident with anyone falling off the mast, so that was something unique to remember too.

It was during this posting that our Marine band was given orders to travel to Faslane Naval Base on the river Clyde about 25 miles from Glasgow.

We were to board a submarine support supply vessel to accompany three Royal Navy submarines and several destroyers, taking part in NATO (North Atlantic Treaty Organization) exercises with the American Navy in the Atlantic Ocean.

The supply ship (or 'tender' as the U.S. Navy call them) was around 20,000 tons so was not small, and had been built by the Americans during WW2 and sold to the British Government.

She creaked and wallowed in the angry waters of the Atlantic, and there were times when we thought we were going down to 'Davy Jones's locker' when huge waves hit her bows and smashed across the decks, but she always came back and heaved herself up above the waterline once more to battle onwards in the raging Atlantic ocean.

We were at sea on these exercises for about 12 days, and in this time the surface ships had the job of trying to find the submerged submarines of both navies, and the destroyers, known as the greyhounds of the sea, would race around in circles pushing up huge white wakes behind them as they went about their business of practicing 'seek and destroy' tactics. We never saw the submarines at all until we eventually reached port at the US Submarine base in New London, Connecticut.

During this time our marine band had done nothing at all except keep out of the way of the crew of the supply ship as they went about their daily sea duties, but as soon as we reached New London we were overloaded with work. Again, our duties were to play music for ceremonial parades on the jetty, and for dinner parties hosted by the British Atlantic Fleet Admiral entertaining his American counterparts.

I think we must have been popular, or just that they liked the British, for the U.S. Navy invited us to go aboard the USS 'Nautilus', the first nuclear powered submarine in the World. It was vast! Nothing like the conventional diesel powered subs of that time; and we were shown most of the spacious interior of the vessel except the top secret nuclear plant.

On the second day we were in port the band was invited by the U.S. Marines Base to a special celebration dance in their barracks, and on arriving there we were gobsmacked to see and hear the U.S. Marine Big swing Band onstage playing really top class music. We had never heard any service band in the UK play as well as they did, and everyone in the band seemed to stand up at one stage or another and play an outstanding solo.

When we arrived, one of the U.S. Marine Corporals in the 'Non swing Marching Band' (so he informed us) said "Hi guys! I hope you like cold beer, not that warm stuff you Limey's drink back home. Just help yourself, for everything is free for you as our guests, tonight."

We were in New London for seven days and during this time we were allowed shore leave. But unlike being in a British port and allowed to wear civilian clothes, our service uniform was mandatory.

It was an immediate attraction to the average American citizen as we walked down a street, and they would stop and shake our hand, saying 'Hi there! You must be British?' After endless encounters I thought it would be a novel idea to stick a notice on my forehead saying 'Before you ask, I'm British!'

One evening I went ashore by myself and walked into a dance club. The doorman told me there was no entry charge for me, since I was welcome as their British guest, so wearing that uniform did have its advantages.

It was called the 'Seven Brothers Restaurant' and I remember that clearly, because five of the brothers had survived military service in WW2 and either ran the restaurant and/or played in the band. They were all of Italian decent, and of course cooked the most wonderful dishes in their establishment.

I just listened to them playing, and when they had said good night to their customers, one of the brothers spotted me sitting at a table. He was down off the bandstand in a flash and shaking my hand. "Hey guys! Looky what we have here – a British Royal Marine!" He was the first and only civilian in that town to recognize exactly what I was!

They were really friendly people, and it turned out they had all been stationed in England for a short duration before being shipped off to U.S. army units driving an offensive against the Germans in Italy, because they all spoke Italian and were invaluable to the army as translators. During their stay in England they had been doing field exercises with Royal Marine Commandos, and therefore knew what all the insignia on my uniform meant.

"So you are a musician? What instrument do you play?" Asked one of the brothers, as he spotted the little brass music lyre on the sleeve of my uniform jacket. When I told them I played the trombone they immediately asked me to bring it in the next night to play with their band, since they had trombone music for me. The reason was that one of the brothers that had been killed in action in Italy had been a trombone player in their band, before being conscripted into the army.

This was the first time I had played with American musicians, and they had a very good collection of great tunes. Far superior to the old dog-eared corny music we had in our Marine dance band collection at the time. It was an exciting experience for a young lad like me, and I enjoyed every minute of playing with that band. Besides playing great tunes, we also had requests coming from the dancers, and one of them asked if 'the trombone player could play Tommy Dorsey's 'I'm getting sentimental over you'.

Now Tommy had died only a few years before, and his famous band was still operational under his brother, Jimmy Dorsey. 'Sentimental over you' was Tommy's signature tune, and any trombone player worth his salt learned to play it, and I was no exception.

It is not hard, but does require many hours of practice to play with a degree of feeling and smoothness, and I knew the tune from memory and so did the brothers.

"You ok with this, Les?' asked the leader, and I said it was fine and just launched straight into the tune as Dorsey used to do. The band immediately caught on to the standard key of 'D' major that Tommy played it in and all went well to the end.

At the end of the tune I was shaking with excitement and the guys in the band could see the glow on my face I guess, for they cheered and said 'how great' it was, and the dancers were clapping. Several drinks arrived on the table besides the bandstand and were consumed by the players, except myself, for I had been put off alcohol by my experience with the cider back in England. Mind you, I made up for that in later years!

After the job was finished and the brothers had packed up their instruments, they told me to follow them into a private part of the club that was their own dining room, and that I was to sit down, as I was going to get a real treat for my efforts on the bandstand.

That was the first time I had ever tasted pizza and it was wonderful, since the American fast food chains had not yet reached Britain. On the last night they gave me a little present in the form of a five dollar bill, and said I had to hang on to this for good luck, since they firmly believed it had got five of them through the war and would help bring good luck to me in the future. They wanted to pay me too, but I refused to take it as I had thoroughly enjoyed my experience of playing music with an American band, and that was payment enough for me.

On the day before our last in New London, the supply ship was opened to the public and many civilians came aboard to visit.

Disaster struck in the late afternoon at high tide when the ship was riding high in the water, and the wooden gangway supplied by the U.S. Dockyard authorities was over loaded with people. The structure could not take all the weight and collapsed, and many people were seriously injured as they fell a long way down from the high gangway into the water, with three people being killed as they hit the side of the dock or the ship.

There was not much we could do except convey our sincere apologies to the injured, and our condolences to the families of the dead. It certainly was not the fault of the Royal Navy or in fact anyone else, for later we heard that on investigation of the broken gangway by the U.S. authorities, they discovered that the wood had been rotting away internally over the years in use. As a consequence of that accident, they withdrew every similar type of gangplank in the U.S. ports from service, and replaced them with new steel structured gangways.

Two days later we arrived in Halifax, Nova Scotia (Canada). I don't recall exactly what we were doing there, for the band was not required to play music, and I suspect it was only a courtesy call, or perhaps to deliver some cargo to the Royal Canadian Navy, but 23 hours later we set Sail for Scotland, and the Holy Loch.

Looking on the Internet, I see that nowadays Halifax is a lovely city and has much to offer, but my recollection of the place back then in the late fifties, was of a rough looking area more akin to a logging town, and it was not popular with the crew, as one had to be over 21 and needed a drinking licence before they would serve you in the local bars.

That was a three day application so a lot of disappointed sailors returned early to the ship, to buy a few small cans of beer from the NAAFI canteen.

Each person over 21 was allowed a tot (measure) of rum issued by the Navy, and up to four cans of light beer per day. No hoarding was allowed, and anyone caught breaking the rules was severely punished and his privileges removed. (I say 'he' for at that time women did not serve aboard Royal Naval vessels and were based in shore establishments).

When my 18 month tour of duty with the Arbroath band was completed, I returned to the Royal Marines School of Music in Deal, Kent, where I spent the next six months just hanging about doing nothing much in particular, except daily practice on my trombone.

I needed nobody to tell me to do it, for by this time I knew it was the only thing I enjoyed doing most. Much better than marching up and down in the band assigned to parade duties, listening to the dulcet sounds of Sgt. Crowther, yelling at the latest batch of new recruits.

Technically speaking, I was awaiting a posting overseas. But the 'draft office' that designated musicians to ships and shore establishments around the World, had not made up their minds just where they wanted to send Musician Weddell.

So I found myself playing in the staff band for a few weeks, which was pretty good, for they were the cream of the musical talent in the School of Music. Trouble was we never got to play more than a few bars of music at any one time, because the Director of Music for the Royal Marines was teaching Senior NCOs to be conductors as part of their music course for further promotion to Bandmaster.

Although I did not have to do so as I was classified as being of a 'satisfactory' standard to play in any band of the Royal Marines, I decided to sneak a few lessons with Professor Hargreaves, who was a Cornet virtuoso and a wonderful brass teacher.

He encouraged me to learn to play in several Clefs, not just the standard Bass Clef taught at that time in basic music lessons to trombone players.

I attended several practise sessions with the Betteshanger colliery brass band as Professor John Hargreaves was the Director of Music. He placed me on the bass trombone parts as they were written in the bass clef, and very soon I was able to read the second trombone, and finally first trombone parts, which are written in treble clef in brass band music.

He also taught me how to read alto and tenor clefs so that I would be prepared for the future, and he was so right, for both these clefs came up in the music I was to play in the future, when I became a temporary member of the Singapore Symphony Orchestra.

I was always doing something musical, for there was a dance band which many of the lads got together to practise in a dis-used shower rooms, the only space we could find without annoying others in our living quarters.

That was fun! We had some old band arrangements which we borrowed from one of the Band Masters in the Music School library, and we had a full compliment of five saxophones, four trombones and four trumpets.

Unfortunately, we had no rhythm section because the drummers did not want to carry the full drum kit over from the concert hall rooms, and there was no piano, or power plug for the electric guitar. But once or twice, one of the string bass players would play with us for a bit of solid rhythm.

But the great day came when I was told I would be joining a new band being sent out to HMS 'Terror,' a land based establishment in Singapore Naval Base. We were allowed two weeks leave before sailing from Greenock docks near Glasgow, and I spent it with my Mother and sister, because my Mum had decided to move back up to Scotland, and live with Jeanette.

That pleased me, because I was worried about leaving her for 18 months, for she was now in her late sixties and retired from work. Dad had long gone, having died of Cancer in the Royal Infirmary in Edinburgh, when I was about 12 years old.

4. *'A life on the ocean wave'*

HMS 'Triumph' cast off her mooring ropes and very slowly started to move away from the dockside. I stood on deck with the rest of the Royal Marines Band bound for the Far East and our new posting in Singapore, all dressed in our best blue uniforms and white pith helmets as we played selections of tunes with a nautical flavour, from Henry Wood's Sea Songs suite.

This was a WW2 Aircraft carrier of the 'Colossus Type, at 13,000 plus weight, with a complement of 1200 when fully loaded with aircraft and servicing crews, and with a capability of 25 knots, which was fast for a ship of her day. So with only a working crew of around 300, and she had no aircraft on board, and was not operational as far as being war ready. Her job now was, to transport thousands of tons of Military equipment and stores around the World to British Bases, including Singapore, her last port of call before returning home to the UK.

It was a typical February morning; Dank, and with that kind of fine rain that can soak you to the skin in no time. The white 'Blanco' liquid that we used to brush onto our helmets to keep them sparkling white, began to run down onto our uniforms, and the Bandmaster looked anxiously in the direction of the deck officer in charge of the 'leaving harbour' parade, who was already dismissing the sailors who had lined the ship's flight deck. He gave the order for us to be dismissed, and we at last started to march towards the huge lift on the deck of the old aircraft carrier, that would take us below decks, and out of the miserable drizzle.

It was a strange feeling for all of us as we were mostly in our late teens, or for some, early twenties. We were leaving our homeland, and it gradually dawned on me that it would be a very long time before I saw the UK again, and my Mother in particular.

As the ship made its way down the River Clyde towards the sea, I looked through one of the portholes on our mess deck. There were a few trees on the far bank, but nothing more conspicuous than that, and grassy fields stretching to the horizon, interrupted now and then by passing vessels navigating up the channel, presumably to the docks that we had just departed from.

We were all feeling a little homesick already, but there was still an air of excitement because we were going on a voyage to places with exotic names, and a final destination in a far away country called Singapore. In our young minds, the very name of the place suggested oriental delights just waiting for us to savour.

On the journey, we would pass through the Suez Canal and call at Trincomalee in Ceylon, (now called Sri Lanka) to refuel. We must have called at other ports on the voyage, but I just cannot remember them, but my memory of 'Trinco' as we all called it, is still vivid even today.

Anchoring in a beautiful natural harbour, we could see the sea life in the clear waters below us as we stood on that high deck. Many flying fish jumped from the water, and on one occasion we had most of the ship's company that was off duty up there, watching a huge Manta Ray swimming gracefully close to the ship.

The land area around the lagoon was covered in a lush green of thick jungle, with colourful birds flying effortlessly from tree to tree. It was sweltering hot tropical weather, but this did not bother us too much, because we had gradually got used to the heat as the ship progressed towards the Suez Canal some weeks before.

That evening we were told we could go ashore, but had to be back on board by 10pm, as the ship would sail promptly at midnight, for it had taken on fuel and was ready to leave. To get ashore we all had to board little cutters or 'bum boats,' to ferry us to the jetty about a quarter of a mile from the vessel.

We were intensely excited; for this was the first time they had allowed the ships' company to go ashore since we had left Gibraltar 12 days before, and there was much laughter as the little boats chugged their way towards the landing jetty.

Beer is the first thing on any sailor's mind when getting ashore, this is of course apart from the company of a pretty woman, and there appeared to be none except for the old ladies trying to sell us things we did not want.

So we looked for the nearest 'watering hole' only to discover the extortionate prices they were asking, and bitterly disappointed, we turned our attention to wandering around the few stalls outside in the dusty street.

The smells and sights of the place hit us, and it did not take long for me to lose interest in the many people trying to sell us wooden statues of elephants and other paraphernalia. With darkness upon us there was nothing to see after the initial short tour of rickety shacks and a few stone built shops, and we were thankful when the boats arrived to take us back to the ship.

Although our trip ashore had been relatively uneventful, we were treated to a rude awaking around 3am as the ship was sailing into international waters, for the skies had lit up in an amazing fireworks display of lightening as the thunder rolled and the tropical rain started pelting down in sheets of seemingly solid water.

The rest of the trip was uneventful as we languished in the bowels of that ship, passing time by playing music a couple of times a week to entertain the ships' company, and playing endless board games such as Monopoly and Chess, besides the usual card games for tots of rum.

In those days, every serving member of the Royal Navy over the age of twenty one was entitled to a 'tot' or measure of three parts water to one part of 100% Jamaican dark rum; a legacy from a grateful Island after the Royal Navy got rid of the pirates that plagued Jamaica at the time.

Myself and several others, were not entitled to a rum issue as we were underage, so we were issued with lime juice, and referred to as 'Limers' by the old sea dogs in the band that were in their twenties and drank the rum. Mind you, that did not stop us 'Limers' from having the occasional taste of the stuff, when friends gave us a little in the bottom of their tin mug. It was risky; for if an Officer witnessed this, both culprits could be in deep trouble.

HMS Triumph had an illustrious history; She spent a great deal of time in Korean waters during the Korean conflict, and if you wish to know more about this ship, you can access all the information on the Internet by inserting the name of the ship in a search engine.

Life on board was a luxury for us, since the ship carried only a small crew. The whole voyage took us six weeks, because we were not travelling at speed. There was no Naval Aircraft on board, so the decks that would normally house them, were full of crated supplies, and a few vehicles, as cargo.

Apart from the restricted places such as the Officers Quarters, engine rooms and the flight deck and the bridge, we practically had the run of the ship. It was vast, and we found it to be a sturdy vessel when we hit rough seas. Our mess deck or living space, was designed to hold a large crew, but we had it all to ourselves as the serving crew on board had the flight crew quarters, as they were more accessible to the many stations on board that had to be manned by the sailors on duty.

The reason the flight deck was out of bounds at sea was because it had no protection rails and anyone could be blown off the open deck. But in port, when it was quiet and the weather usually nice, we were allowed to go up there on the flight deck and exercise by walking around, playing music, or even giving one of our impromptu concerts of playing music for the ships' crew, which was always appreciated.

As there was only a small crew the Navy catering staff on board had a lighter work load and thus seemed to excel themselves in providing us all with superb meals, and as it was a large ship, there was a large cafeteria, that could accommodate a full ship's compliment, and we had it all to ourselves because there could not have been more than 300 in the crew, including the Band.

It was great, because it meant no washing up to do. When you got in line for your food you simply grabbed a tray which had compartments pressed into it for various foods, and a set of knife, fork, and spoon, then after loading up your tray with your choice of food you found a table and sat down to eat. After the meal, you simply put the tray (dispensing with any leftover food into a bin provided for the purpose) in a slot on a container rack, and the knives and forks into a deep stainless steel container ready for it to be wheeled into an automatic dishwashing machine.

This was a luxury, as we found out much later when we had to go on a small Frigate named HMS 'Alert' which was the Flag Ship of the Admiral of the Far East.

The mess deck quarters on that ship were tiny, and it had no cafeteria. We had a 'mess' table and had to go to the galley and bring back the food for our Band in hot containers, then serve it up at the table. Oh, and yes; all the pots had to be scrubbed clean by those unfortunates in the Band who had the duty of food server for the day.

5.

'Singapore; Gateway to the mystical Far East'

Waking up one morning, we discovered that HMS Triumph had docked alongside a jetty, and that we had finally arrived at the Royal Naval Base at Sembawang, in Singapore. It had been just over six weeks since we had set sail from Greenock Docks in Glasgow. Gathering all our equipment together, we were taken by bus and truck to our new home in HMS Terror, the land based headquarters of the Commander in Chief of the British Far East Fleet.

We were to be his new band; playing for all official parades, and formal occasions, for both the Admiral and his distinguished guests. He turned out to be a very nice man who loved music, and was most complimentary when we were required to perform.

A few of us became involved with playing with the Singapore Symphony Orchestra, of which our Admiral was one of the patrons.

For several weeks we had been rehearsing stolidly for the performance of Handel's 'Messiah' and on the big day of the performance, we discovered that a last minute order had come in for our Marine band to play for a cocktail party aboard the frigate HMS 'Alert'.

Our bandmaster was aware of the problem, but said duty had to come first and he was sorry, but there was nothing he could do about it. As we sat in our chairs on the jetty in the coolness of the evening playing music for the guests mingling on the large quarterdeck of the 'Alert', we became increasingly more worried that we were going to miss the concert, for time was quickly passing by and we had to be there ready to play at 8pm.

To this day I don't know how he found out, but the Admiral appeared suddenly on the gangway of the ship and whispered something to one of his officers, who hurriedly walked down to our Bandmaster and told him to dismiss the band. Not only that, but there was a Navy bus waiting at our quarters to take us into Singapore to the Victoria Halls to play on the Concert.

We changed out of our uniforms and into our white sharkskin tuxedo jackets on the way, and arrived only five minutes before the concert, much to the relief of the Conductor, for we constituted the majority of his brass section.

It did not take long for us to settle into our new home and established a routine that was to last for the duration of our stay, or as the American Military call it, Tour of Duty, which was usually 18 months, playing music on the morning parades when the flag was raised, exactly at 8am.

After this was finished, we would go to breakfast, and according to whatever we had been allocated to do, we cleaned our quarters and reported to the mess hall that doubled as our band practice room.

But getting used to the heat took some time, and many of us suffered sunburn and exhaustion from not drinking enough water. This was rectified on the second week when the M.O. (Medical Officer) addressed all new arrivals in the mess hall. We were told to drink plenty of water and lime juice in particular, which we would find at all times available in jugs in the bar in the NAAFI Canteen. (Navy, Army, Air force Institute) It was free, so there was no excuse for anyone not taking enough liquid.

It must have been a pain in the side of the cooking staff, that would have enough work to do preparing breakfast, lunch, dinner, and cleaning up the cooking pots and the kitchen, without adding the task of topping up pitchers of water and lime juice. And men, being messy, there were always mopping up to be done around the tables from spilt juice on the floor.

The barrack accommodation was excellent, having high ceilings with large bamboo shuttered doors and windows that allowed a good circulation of air, making for a comfortable sleep in the high humidity of the tropical nights. We found out that during the Japanese occupation of Singapore in WW2, the Japanese Navy had used the dockyard, and billeted their sailors in the same accommodation we were using.

There were quite a lot of sailors billeted in the blocks next to ours, for the camp was primarily used as a transit centre for ship crews arriving from, and returning, to the UK.

This was usually done by the RAF flying them out from the UK or other British bases abroad, to land in RAF Changi. Then they would be bussed over the Island to the Naval Base, and via HMS Terror, processed for medical requirements (inoculations, issue of Tropical kit, and a period of four or five days to try and adjust to the heat) then taken to the ship that would be their home for the next 18 months.

Often the crews being relieved could be in the Barracks at HMS Terror at the same time as their replacements that had just arrived, and there would be conflicts in the bar, when the cheap ale had flowed freely for an hour or so in an evening.

Thankfully, this was not often, as it meant the Commanding Officer would have to issue a directive that the pub remain closed, certainly until the crew leaving for the UK had departed to RAF Changi, or to Singapore Airport, for their flight home on schedule civilian flights to the UK.

Frivolity reigned in the evenings after the NAAFI canteen and bar closed at 10.30pm, and the aroma of Asian food bought from the enterprising locals that ran two stalls outside on the public road, soon wafted through the air in the living quarters.

It was not a difficult life, as we did practically nothing all day, and thinking back, I believe this could be the motivation for some people to do strange things to pass the time. We all soon discovered the bus services inside the (then) very large Naval Base, and to the City center of Singapore, and most afternoons when we were not onboard a ship travelling to some official engagement in Hong Kong or Manila, or other South Asia country, we were allowed 'all night leave' which means you could stay out of barracks until 7.30am the following morning, but must be back on duty ready to do morning parade by 7.45am.

This really was a luxury, for it was like a paid holiday! Some of the band members were married, and had brought their wives and children out from the UK free of charge, courtesy of the Forces, and lived in, or just off, the camp, in either married quarters, or rented housing. This included the Band Sergeant, who had two kids, and often would invite a couple of us to come to the BBQ in his back garden.

The only condition he stipulated was, for us to bring beer! That was not a problem, as it was cheap enough in the NAAFI canteen at a special discount for the armed forces. Those attending the affair would club together and buy a carton or two of canned 'Tiger' beer and take them to the BBQ either by using a Naval Base taxi, or a car, belonging to one of the guys in the band.

I remember a good pal of mine named Patrick Flynn, nicknamed 'Errol' after the film star Errol Flynn, who bought an old Nash sedan car. I still remember the smell of polished leather seats; the large interior it had, and those small windows like we saw in the period vehicles used by the bad guys in gangster movies of the 1920's.

Pat's car had a big engine, that I do remember, and Patrick was pretty savvy at fixing it when it stopped, which was often, from some ailment in the engine department, usually from the distributor cap and/or wiring or setting of the gaps in the plugs.

We were both in the Singapore Symphony orchestra, which sounds like the big time (it is today, because Singapore has a world class orchestra) but back fifty plus years ago, it was a combination of amateur players only. Patrick was a wonderful pianist and he was often featured as the soloist on one of the concerts, playing a Piano Concerto.

Here is a website that explains better than I can, how my old pal Patrick Flynn turned out;   http://www.exroyalmarinesbandsmen.net/Flynn.htm

I will always have a memory of seeing Patrick sitting behind the driving wheel in that old car of his in Singapore, when we were both vibrant young lads full of life and raring to get out of those barrack gates, and whizz down the twisting roads to the city centre of Singapore for a concert, or to part our ways outside the Britannia Club, a haven for British servicemen.

One could get a fantastic haircut and shave from three or four Indian guys, who would give your scalp and face a good massage with bay rum! Then it was upstairs to the half open bar for a pint of cold Tiger beer, and look at the people swimming in the large pool below.

Of course, Singapore is totally different nowadays. It is larger, has one of the best underground train services in the World, and is so much cleaner and healthier to live in for the locals. It is now a World leader in education and medical facilities.

Back in my day, it was open sewers which were as big as canals, and when it had not rained for several weeks, there was a dreadful pong in the air, and everyone sighed with relief when the monsoons came.

That meant downpours, that were so strong they could hurt your head, hence the term Tropical downpour, I think. Those monsoon drains would fill in no time and you would see brown coloured water rapidly flowing down towards the sea, and in it flotsam of all sorts; from trees, old prams, dead dogs and other animals, and even the remains of stillborn babies, or even a body of someone who had committed suicide, or had been murdered.

At that time I was being paid a decent wage in the services, and I decided it was time to buy myself a new trombone. The Selmer had been a good start, but now that I was in my mid twenties, I was playing with more experience, and had the need for something a bit better, and decided to go into the city and find a musical instrument shop.

There were no doubt several music shops in Singapore at that time, but I decided to stick with the one I found that sold brass and reed instruments. I cannot recall the name of the shop, but they had a brand new King 2B in the window, just sitting in the open case. I got to try it, and made a deposit of roughly half the price of the instrument and would call back in a week or two when I had the rest of the money.

It was a lovely instrument and so much lighter than my Selmer trombone, which I continued to use on parade band, not wanting the slide section of my new King to get ruined by the dust from the parade ground. That instrument lasted me until I got the job in Radio and Television Singapore orchestra, and I decided to sell it, and buy a new King 3B trombone, which has a larger bell, and to me, a bigger sound.

I had found the right trombone for me, and that was to last me for the next twenty years or so, until I was living in Blackpool and working with big bands. Then in a position to experiment, I bought a Yamaha tenor trombone with two slides, then a Conn Constellation, which as a lovely instrument, but a bit heavy for me. I went to an Urbie Green Concert and was bedazzled by his fantastic talent, and decided to order a Martin trombone of the same model as Urbie uses.

The one thing I discovered about trombones was, that, 'what is good for someone else, may not be good for you.' The Martin was too light for me, and so I sold the three trombones and bought a brand new King 3B, which turned out to be the best trombone for the kind of jobs I was being hired to do, all along!

It took me a long time to realize that you must find the right instrument and size mouthpiece, that suits you, as well as the kind of work you do most. If you are going to be playing classical music then you want a big bore trombone, and perhaps one with an extended F attachment, and a large mouthpiece.

If on the other hand, you are playing as a solo trombone in a jazz band you can use a tenor trombone with a smaller bell, and if you play in a dance orchestra/big band or brass band, you can use such as the King 3B or other make, with a medium sized bell. It really is an individual thing; if you are not sure about anything, then seek the advice of a good trombone teacher.

Meanwhile, back in Singapore....

But there were many good things to see which I used to enjoy; and one of them was walking down 'change alley' which is a tourist attraction today.

The original passageway was a shortcut from Raffles Place, to Collyer Quay, and was famous for changing money of all international denominations, and a place where you could pick up a bargain, if you knew what to look for. Today, the alley is slightly larger, and more commercial, and it is safer for tourists to buy momentums of Singapore and the Far East.

Another favourite attraction for me, was the Haw Par Villa which back in the 1960's, was still named Tiger Balm gardens. It contains some wonderful statues of Chinese mythological figures and a fine collection of plants and flowers, including beautiful orchids, of many colours and varieties.

Today it is easy to reach, as there is an MRT (Mass Rapid Transportation) underground rail station on the circle line which is right in the vicinity of Haw Par Villa.

For dining, there is a fine selection of wonderful cafés and restaurants to choose from. I recall one of my favourite dishes was Singapore chilli crab. The place to eat was not a fancy establishment, but a small open air café right on the end of a wooden pier in Bedok, an outlying district village at that time, right next to the sandy beach.

Freshly caught mud crabs were cleaned and boiled in chilli sauce and other tasty ingredients, and it was a lip smacking, shell crunching experience, and you were given the use of a small hammer and a large clean towel to cover your clothes, or put around your neck. It was all washed down with either an ice cold beer, or your choice of a soft drink. There are plenty of such crab café's in that area in the Singapore of today.

Despite the name of chilli crab, it was not so hot that it burned your mouth. I would describe it as a tingling sensation that was enjoyable. There was a wonderful choice of other seafood in that café too, a favourite of the locals who used to patronise it daily. Giant prawns that were as large as Langoustines in the UK, and there will always be questions about if they are called Tiger Prawns, Dublin Bay Prawns, or Crayfish. Believe me, whatever they are called, those are large prawns by name in Singapore, and are delicious.

This is not a recipe book, so if your mouth is beginning to water at the thought of something as exotic as Singapore chilli crab, or curry prawns, then I suggest you either go online and order such a dish from your nearest take out shop, or learn to cook the dishes yourself.

There are plenty of good recipes on Google and other search engines, which you can copy, and try for yourself. The good thing about oriental food is that most of the ingredients are usually cheap to buy, and with the advent of oriental stores and even some giant supermarkets, the ingredients are available the World over.

HMS 'Terror' was actually a transit camp; because it served the purpose of housing men off the ships, that came into the Naval dockyard for quick re-fits, or change of crews. The men would be transferred to the barracks, and leave the next day for the airport for a flight home to the UK, or stay in the quarters for as long as it took the dockyard to complete the necessary repairs to their vessel, and then they would go back aboard, and take it out for sea trials.

So there was a constant flow of personnel into and out of the barracks, and young men soon get bored when they find themselves with 'nothing to do' after the pub (NAAFI canteen bar) has closed at 10.30pm, and jumping in the swimming pool fully clothed became boring, so they would dream up something else to amuse themselves. This was carried out even when they knew there was a duty MP patrol around the camp and of course this made it more thrilling not to get caught.

One morning there was a commotion as one of our lads entered the room laughing his head off. "Hey, you ought to see what is up the flagpole! Somebody has raised a pair of pink knickers, and the C. O. (Commanding Officer) is going berserk because they can't get them down as the ropes are twisted!"

Morning parade went on as usual and the offending ladies delicates were still fluttering in the breeze on the pole. Instead of facing 'that' flagpole we had on this occasion to look at a temporary pole and flag they had rustled up from the stores. It was several hours before they got a mobile crane in and removed the offending bloomers and restored life to normal.

The outcome of it all was that they never did find out who the culprit was and neither did we, although we had our suspicions, for there were a couple of real jokers in the sailors transit block.

We had a marvellous swimming pool in the grounds and made good use of it every day that we were free from duties. To reach it we had to walk down several pathways surrounded by long grass that seemed to grow back as fast as they could cut it. We had been warned to look out for wildlife, for there are unsavoury things like huge centipedes and other insects that can give you a nasty bite, including lizards and reptiles.

Usually we stuck to the footpaths, but on one occasion one of the sailors decided to take a short cut through the long grass to his living quarters and was bitten by a snake. He had the foresight to remember what it looked like and described it to the camp Doctor who recognized it from a chart and administered the right antidote serum to save his life.

It turned out the reptile was a grass viper, and it was lucky the lad had not been far away from the camp sick bay (hospital) and got the treatment within only minutes of being bitten.

That was serious enough for the C.O. To order everyone to assemble in the mess halls and have the Doctor lecture us on reptiles and the effect of their poisons, and no one strayed from the footpaths ever again.

After a few months of getting to know the place we could name the bus services and roads that went from the Naval base into the main city centre of Singapore, and we began to explore that wonderful place to the utmost.

Today Singapore is a wealthy Republic and an entirely different place from 50 years ago when I served my time in HMS Terror, for in those days there had been little change from the colonial days of British rule.

Government departmental structure and business were set up the way the British had run it for decades, and although a start had been made by the new Government of Singaporeans to make radical changes running the country and creating housing for everyone along with education for all children, and improving health and care facilities, much had still to be done to take away the poverty and provide the people of Singapore with full employment and the foundation for a happy and healthy life.

It was a big project and took several decades to perfect. Because of this new Nation's diligence, today every child goes to school, and gets a first class education in the key skills that will ensure a decent future for them.

Everyone speaks good English as well as their own native tongue, and the vibrant Republic of Singapore competes in the international business market with considerable force and expertise.

6. *'On a slow boat to China'*

One day, our Bandmaster told us we were going to Hong Kong. The British Far East Fleet was to take part in a SEATO (South East Asia Treaty Organization) sea exercise with other nations, and we had to go aboard a ship and sail with the fleet. At the end of these actions, all the ships of the navies involved would be meeting in Hong Kong, and our job was to provide music on ceremonial parades and for official receptions and dinner parties on board HMS 'Alert', an old frigate from WW2 days, used by our Admiral, Sir Charles Lamb, for his headquarters when he was away from Singapore. The ship they put us on for the transit was HMS Concord, a fast destroyer. Her top speed was 36 knots, which is roughly 40 MPH and very fast for a seagoing vessel of her time. She went into service too late to combat the U-boats in the Atlantic, but served in the Far East for ten years. In 1949 she was involved in the rescue of the sloop, Amethyst rescue. Later, she went on to serve during the Korean War. When we eventually reached port after the sea exercises, we left Concord and boarded HMS Alert, which was docked almost along side her.

It usually took us five days to sail to HK and the Admiral would only come aboard for his official dinner parties, as he would fly by a Royal Air Force plane from Singapore to Hong Kong, and stayed at the British Governor's official residence. However, for official ceremonies and dinners he would come aboard his ship, and we would be in demand to play music as required.

After our duties were over we were allowed shore leave, and on the first day in Port we met some musicians from an American warship, and discovered a friendly bar that would allow us to play live music. We all returned to our ships and brought our instruments back to the bar, and had a great jazz session.

We arranged to meet these American lads the next day to take them on board our ship and treated them to our rum (by now all us 'Limers' had turned twenty one and were entitled to a rum issue) ration, and the American sailors were looking forward to it immensely, since their Navy (was at that time) 'dry' with no alcohol on board.

The next day came and only one American turned up, and he had tears in his eyes as he told us that President Kennedy had been assassinated in Dallas. We felt just as bad, because Kennedy was also popular in the UK, as a dynamic World leader.

The visit to Hong Kong was cut short, and that evening the American fleet left the harbour, and we sailed the following morning, to return to Singapore.

It turned out that we were to make numerous trips to Hong Kong on this old vessel, and it was a new experience every time we set foot aboard the old tub. She was forever breaking down in the China Sea, which is not an ideal place to be wallowing for hours, whilst the engineers toiled with fixing new bearings to the drive shaft, or whatever it was that caused the breakdown.

Storms came and went quickly, and the weather could be violent enough to make the ancient structure of HMS 'Alert' creak and shudder as the vessel laboured through the huge waves. I was lucky enough to be a pretty good sailor which is something I could not say about several of the lads in the band. And, it was rumoured by the crew that even the Captain of the ship was prone to sea sickness.

During these storms nobody wanted to eat food, but the cook still went ahead and provided some form of nourishment for those that did want to eat. I recall that this chap was a bit of a joker, and loved nothing better than to make the poor souls in the crew suffering from sea sickness feel even worse in a storm, by leaving a piece of pork cracking to burn on the hot plate!

The pungent smell would soon make its way down the air ducts and into the mess decks and men would be rushing for the heads (naval term for latrines) or to the upper deck, to vomit over the side. It was only when the smell hit the officer's quarters that he was admonished, and told to get rid of the offending crackling. These days, absolutely nothing is deposited into the ocean, as all British Naval ships store waste until they get to a Port, and taken away by waste removal facilities.

There is no absolute cure for seasickness, and there are many so-called remedies; such as drinking lots of water and keeping on deck in the fresh air, an exercise that is almost impossible on a heaving deck, and prohibited in the Navy except for personnel on duty. Even then, those sturdy sailors wear life jackets and are secured by a line to a safety rail.

Remedies were available that were supposed to relieve sea sickness, but in those days my friends told me they didn't seem to do much good, and the best way they found to combat the 'illness' was to keep a bucket handy, and climb into your hammock, for the duration of the storm.

Any sailor who has used a hammock will tell you it is amongst the most comfortable ways of sleeping on a heaving ship. If you make it up properly with a mattress designed specifically for the purpose, and ensure the ropes are tight enough and secure to the bulkhead stanchions, you will have a most pleasant and relatively trouble free sleep during storms at sea.

On one goodwill visit, we went to Saigon, the Capitol of Vietnam; it was just at the time the French were in the stages of leaving the country. On our visit as part of a large SEATO Navies exercise of what really was a show of force, Saigon was still a tranquil city, with beautiful French style boulevards and clean streets.

There were brightly chequered clothed tables outside every café on the wide pavements, and happy people walking up and down the sidewalks or sitting in rickshaws being transported around the streets. Many of the locals wore the traditional tall peaked straw hats and colourful pyjamas-like silk trouser suits.

HMS Alert tied up alongside the dock next to a very old French aircraft carrier, that was loading stores and military personnel to repatriate to France, and there was no indication whatsoever of the dreadful turmoil that was to soon engulf that beautiful country, in the form of the Vietnam War.

I ended up in a French military hospital with an eye infection because I had been drinking moonshine booze (unknown to me, of course, at the time) with some local friends in a shady bar back in Singapore, a few days before we sailed. It did not affect my friends, but I started to experience the symptoms of infection on the second day of our stay in Saigon, and the medic (we did not have a doctor on our ship unless the Admiral was aboard) immediately arranged for me to be transferred to the French Military Hospital.

I was there for five days, and in this time HMS 'Alert' had left port and sailed for Singapore, and home to HMS 'Terror', our land based Naval establishment.

The band took care of my belongings and put them in my locker in the barracks when they got back to Singapore, and told me later that they were all a bit worried as to my health, and what would happen to me.

They had cause to worry, for I had no passport as we did not normally carry these documents, as they were in the safe keeping of the 'administration' in the Singapore Naval Base. We had our dog tags, of course, and a sort of identity card, showing we were in the Royal Marines, but that was all.

The day came when the French Doctor told me via an interpreter that I could leave the hospital, and I was taken by car to the British Consulate, and they contacted the

Royal Air Force, for they had several flights a week in and out of Saigon to Singapore and elsewhere in the Orient.

So I was taken to the airport and handed over to the RAF flight crew of a Bristol Freighter, a rather ancient cargo aircraft and I was smuggled aboard by the crew, that gave me a large Forces mail bag to carry, and told me to don the RAF cap they loaned me, and just 'act normal' walking to the aircraft from a hanger!

Imagine that happening today? I think not, but back in those times everything was changing rapidly in Vietnam, and security was not as it is today. I eventually got back to HMS Terror barracks, to find myself standing on the carpet in front of the Camp Commander on charges of 'rendering myself unfit for duty' by drinking illicit alcohol!

I was lucky really, for they only stopped two days pay, and confined me to barracks for seven days, and could have charged me if they had wanted to, with the cost of being transported back to Singapore by the RAF. But it was still a good visit for the first two days until I developed the eye problem, and after the splendid lunch our French hosts had provided, they took us to see their equestrian quarters, and a fantastic display of thoroughbred horses going through their paces, and my thoughts went right back to those wonderful days as a young child on that Scottish Farm.

7. *'Meanwhile, back on the Farm'*

As an ex cavalryman, my father knew a thing or two about horses; and that was one of the prime reasons that Mr Cummings, the owner of Dodridge farm, took him on to work. He was in charge of the four Clydesdales workhorses used to pull the ploughs, harrows, corn thresher, and other heavy-duty equipment used on the land.

They were huge gentle beasts, with long tails and shaggy hair hanging down from the flanks of the neck, and with bushy white hair looking comically like gaiters on the bottom of their legs. The ticklish feeling of their soft pink lips gently nibbling sugar lumps from my hand, is an experience that still lingers with me to this day.

I would be about eight years of age when my dad first took me out to the fields with the great beasts. This was just before the tractor started being introduced to the land, and I remember sitting up there on the back of one of the horses, leaving the farmyard, and walking out to the field to be ploughed that day.

I could feel the muscles of the animal bulging beneath my bottom as he walked along, and although it was an awful long way down to the ground, the experience of being a small boy up there on that great broad back, was exhilarating. Dad would say 'Right son –jump!' and would catch me as I came down off the horse, before he hitched the team up to the plough rig. Then he would yell 'yup, yup, Ginger!" to the lead horse, and the team of four great Clydesdale horses would start to pull the plough through the corn stubble.

All four animals had names of course; Billy, Ginger, Smithy, and big Grey. Although they were docile enough, it was wise not to get too close to them, because they could be clumsy. Anything that spooked them, could have all four moving about nervously whinnying, and if your foot happened to be in the way, you stood a good chance of getting near to a quarter ton of prime horse on it!

Those men and women responsible for milking cows and feeding the animals were usually in the animal sheds by 4am; but work outdoors only began when there was enough daylight. This would vary according to the seasons, from around 5am to 8 am. My father would lead the four horses out of the stables into the yard where they would stand quietly, whilst he mumbled sweet nothings in their ear and harnessed them up. Then he would be off to the fields, maybe a mile away from the main buildings, to start the long day of ploughing.

As soon as he had hitched up to the plough, and lined the team up facing the direction he wanted to go, Dad would pull on the lever that lowered the four gleaming 'V' shaped steel plough shafts into the golden stubble of the corn field, and shout his 'yup, yup, boys, let's go!' Those horses knew the routine, for they would start pulling effortlessly on the plough rig as they walked forwards into the field.

On the return trip, the horses would rarely vary from the newly ploughed furrows, resulting in straight rows that would make a Sergeant Major proud. Sea birds would appear as if from nowhere in their dozens, all swooping in circles around the back of the plough as it exposed the rich brown soil, offering them the opportunity of a free feed on fat, juicy, earthworms.

The view of the rolling countryside was breathtaking. With the patchwork of colours of golden corn stubble, green pastures of rich grass, in which contented cows and sheep grazed, the vegetable crops of beetroot, turnips, carrots, onions, Kale, cabbage and potatoes and broccoli, all contrasting with the deep brown of freshly turned earth. Beetroot was grown widely on many farms, and harvested to produce not only a salad, but a scarce commodity in war time, sugar.

Centuries old hedges separated the fields that gently sloped away down into the valley towards the majestic Pencaitland hills in the distance. And above all this tranquil and panoramic beauty, the wonderful scent of wild honeysuckle and primrose flowers, blended with a hint of fresh sea air from the coast just a few miles away, making you want to fill your lungs to the maximum, and celebrate the exhilarating joy of just being alive.

But the days of the horse on the farms were numbered, for the tractor was coming in. A job that could take a team of horses a day to do, could now be done in half a day or less, with a tractor as it did not need to stop and rest. And the driver took his sandwiches with him and a flask of tea, stopping for less time on his 'dinner' break, and could therefore finish the job in hand, and move onto the next one in the same day. Intensive labour costs money, and the more production the farmer could get by using mechanised equipment to reduce these costs, the better turnover he could make by the end of each year.

My father was not keen on the tractor replacing his horses, but had no choice but to learn to drive a tractor and use the equipment that came with it. The alternative would mean him handing in his notice, and having to move away and find another job.

I recall the day a rented brand new Combine harvester arrived on the farm, and the specially trained driver that came with it, wasted no time setting it up in the corn field. Everyone had turned out to see this red monster in use, and we marvelled at the speed at which it worked, and the quality of the bales of hay it deposited behind it ready for collecting and stacking. British farming would never be the same again, for the new mechanised agricultural era had begun.

The large, old-fashioned cast iron cooking stove in our kitchen was a wonder of engineering in the '40's, because it was reliable and sturdy, and housed not only a roaring wood fire that heated the water boiler as well as the house, but ample sized hobs, on which pots and cauldrons could simmer away for days. There was even a facility to place the flat iron to heat up for use when Mother or our sister decided to iron our clothes.

And there were two great ovens at the front of the stove with heavy cast iron doors. In those ovens Mum would bake her bread, scones and cakes, pastries, roasts and stews, and of course those oh, so memorable Christmas Dinners. I remember the gleaming brass handles that she used to open with a couple of dish clothes because they were invariably too hot to open with the bare hand. Dad bypassed it all by using the fire poker to knock the handles upwards and open the doors.

Once a week my mother would spend a good hour cleaning and black leading that cooker until it shone like new. Where she found the time to do it, was beyond me, for she was always cleaning the house and making beds, scrubbing floors or cooking, and still found time to feed the poultry in our garden and do a little weeding in her flower patch in the summer months.

Laundry day was every Friday, no matter what the weather was like. Mum would start around 6.30am by entering the laundry room and building a fire in the grate under the copper cauldron, in which all the clothes were boiled in water containing bleach, to get them spotlessly clean. This was in an out-shed parallel with the kitchen door, and made it a little easier for her to make the many trips back and forth into the cottage.

Filling the copper with water to about half way up, she would place the wooden cover on it and return to the kitchen, and cook breakfast for my father and sister before they went off to work. Cyril and I were allowed to sleep in until 7.30am. We then had to wash, dress in our school clothes, eat breakfast and be on our way with the other farm children at 8.15.

Then she would really start work. I know this, for both my brother and myself helped her in the school holidays. She would clear away all the breakfast things and wash the plates and cups, stowing them in their racks. Then off she would go to the washroom again to check on the temperature of the water. If it was ready, she would add the clothes according to type, all the sheets and shirts and other whites first. Adding bleach and soap flakes to the water, she would replace the lid and retire to the kitchen for a well earned cup of tea and a cigarette. Coffee was almost none existent in Britain in the early 1940's, but there was a substitute made with chicory and/ or acorns, which tasted vile to me. Some people actually got used to drinking a coffee from a bottle, called 'Camp' coffee, but we mostly drank tea, if we could get it, that is. One pot of tea would go a long way, and the tea used perhaps twice, if it still produced a decent cup of the brew.

Then Mum would go back to the wash house for another inspection to check on progress; and if the washing was going to her satisfaction, she would grab hold of a pair of large wooden tongs, and start transferring the clothes into a brown coloured earthenware sink. Adding some of the hot water from the copper, she would then begin to scrub the clothes on a corrugated washing board; rubbing them vigorously up and down, until she was satisfied they were clean.

The next stage was to place them in the tin bath-tub until she had refilled the sink with hot water from a huge cast iron kettle she lugged in from her kitchen. That thing weighed a ton to me, for I could barely lift it, never mind carry it.

But like most healthy farm wives, hard work was no stranger to my Mother, or having to lift heavy weights, that many town women would not even contemplate.

Vigorous rinsing under running cold water ensured that all the soap had been removed, before being transferred once again to the washed out and rinsed tin bath, for the next operation.

Stage three was the mangle. An old fashioned contraption mounted on a cast iron frame with two large rollers engaged by three cogs, all motivated by turning a large master wheel by hand, as each garment was fed carefully through the rollers to extract as much water as possible. This operation was carried out at least twice, sometimes three times, if the garment was large.

Then the galvanised bath in which we all bathed was put to yet another use, when Mum would fill it with the newly washed clothes and then carry it out to the washing lines in the garden, to be pegged up in the clean air. In winter, she paced the washing so that the amount was less each week, and this could be hung in the kitchen annex to dry.

Add to this workload, all the ironing and folding that had to be done when the clothes were dry, and the placing of every item in the correct drawers for each member of the family. All through wash day she would be singing away to herself, or to a popular tune on the radio that could be heard from the house, when the kitchen door was left open in warm weather.

Today, people would shudder to even think about hanging washing up in the kitchen area, but in those far off days there was no alternative to this unhealthy habit.

All the things we now take for granted such as purpose fitted kitchens with all the labour saving devices and refrigerators, dishwashers, automatic washing machines, and clothes dryers, would not come to Britain for the masses until the early nineteen sixties. Everything was as it had been since the Victorian era, until the advent of the government post war re-building programme that created thousands of new homes to replace those flattened by the Luftwaffe.

One day, my father decided that ironing was a simple thing to do, and had a go at ironing one of his shirts when Mum and Jeanette were away visiting friends in one of the farm cottages. On their return, he got a real earwigging, because he had got the iron too hot, and it had left a perfect brown impression of the iron on his clean shirt. I recall his guilty look, and both Cyril and myself laughing at his expense. From then onwards he left the ironing to the women.

Mother was not a tall person, but she was certainly strong. She can best be described as being slightly on the plump side, yet not fat, because she constantly worked all day in the house and garden, and in addition to this, when necessary, she would help out with all the other farm wives in the fields pulling up carrots, turnips, potatoes, cabbages and other essential root vegetables, and also with gathering in the crop harvest in the months of July/August.

Hoeing was a job that everyone hated. But it had to be done, to ensure a full and healthy crop of first class produce. The mechanical technology was there even in those days, but the average farmer could not afford to buy the expensive equipment that was designed to do this job behind a team of horses or a tractor.

So every pair of hands was gratefully welcomed to the hoeing. Sister Jeanette, Cyril, myself, and all the other kids, including the farmer's children and his wife, plus all the women and any visiting friends or relatives to the farm, were all pressed into service. It was not long before we had huge blisters on or thumbs and fingers fro the friction of moving the wooden handle.

Anyone who is a gardener will know how back breaking this can be to remove weeds and other unwanted growth between tightly planted vegetables; for even though you have a hoe, you spend a lot of time bending over, to remove something that can only be done by hand. If you can, try to imagine converting the average sized domestic vegetable garden into several large fields, you will get some idea of the backbreaking exhaustion at the end of a very long day.

Even when Mother was supposed to be having a short break, she would be thinking of something to do; planning the evening meal, maybe changing the curtains, or what shopping errands she needed to do in the village three miles away.

On those trips she used her trusty bicycle, the type with the wicker basket fixed to the front of the handlebars. It was a fairly uneventful journey down hill all the way to the village, but the return journey was laborious, as it was up a long steep incline, and we all discovered the best way was to dismount, and push the cycle most of the way home.

Yet despite all the hard work, she was to live a full life for another thirty years before she finally left this World at the grand old age of 82.

Today, in 2015, farming in the western world is big business; they now use giant multi-wheeled tractors with a variety of fitted hydraulic contraptions that can perform different functions. Most of these new vehicles have a self-contained weatherproof cabin for the operator, that often includes heat, a stereo radio, and on some models, even a mobile phone facility.

In the vast farmlands of Canada and the United States of America, they use massive high tech vehicles that are aided by GPS satellite tracking to ensure absolutely straight furrows when ploughing, or straight lines for the state of the art combined harvesters for scooping up and processing corn, wheat and barley. Anything up to ten in a row of these agricultural monsters can gulp up many miles of crops in just one day.

Back in the 1940's there was only one man and his horses; or at best, the use of the newly introduced tractor. It was a revolution at the time, but there was no fancy heated cab for protection from the elements when the rain came down in sheets, or in the freezing cold of winter months.

On the odd occasions when Father took myself and Cyril to work with him out into the fields, probably more for a bit of company than anything else, he would stop working for about ten minutes, usually about 11 am. He would take the large bucket of water swinging from the back of his seat on the plough, lift off the heavy wood cover, and give each of the horses a drink.

They would try to nudge his arm out of the way to get into his jacket pocket, because they knew he carried sugar lumps in there, that he gave to them as a treat now and again. We would then sit down on a grass bank, and rest. Cyril and I would have our little bottles of water and a 'piece' (a jam sandwich) that mum had prepared for us, whilst Dad would have a woodbine and a drink of his tea, from a coal miner's enamel jug. The lid served as a cup as well as an airtight cover, that clamped down over the jug with a metal clasp to keep the contents hot.

Then off we would go again until 2pm, when Dad would arrive at the end of a furrow and unhitch the horses and let them feed from their nosebags. We did the same; for either my sister or mother, would appear with a cheery "Hello boys - are you ready to eat?" A basket full of wholesome food would be opened and spread onto a tablecloth on the grassy bank, and we would all sit and talk whilst we enjoyed the wonderful food, and the marvellous view for half an hour. That meal could be made up of home baked bread, home made butter, a piece of cheese with some home made pickles, or perhaps hard boiled chicken eggs with home made mayonnaise, or home made preservative, such as black-current, or strawberry jam.

It was a simple meal, and suffice to fill us up. Meat was a rationed commodity, and we had that on weekends, or chicken, and now and again, roast duck or turkey.

The idyllic scene of man and horse lasted not for very long after that, for the tractor soon replaced them and the gentle giants were retired to pasture. For the remaining years I lived on Dodridge farm, I made it a point to visit my four faithful old friends at least a couple of times a week.

Living on a farm in those days had its compensations, for we often had extras that city and town folks could not have. There was the garden behind the cottage that was more the size of a small field, in which we grew every conceivable vegetable and fruit, as well as keeping a few chickens and geese.

However, like everyone else in the Country, we had a ration book issued to us for essentials such as red meat and sugar. The sight of a banana or an orange was a rare treat. They only appeared every couple of months or so because of the scarcity of supply, thanks to Hitler's U-boats sinking merchant ships bringing supplies to war torn Britain.

You might think that living on a farm would mean you had an endless supply of beef, lamb and pork. Not so. This was strictly controlled by a Government official who made weekly visits to all the farms in the area, meticulously listing all the animals in ledgers.

When any livestock was waiting to be taken to the abattoir, they were counted and immediately taken away in the official Ministry of Agriculture trucks to government depots, to be prepared and distributed into the national food chain. So like everyone else in the Nation, all the Mothers had to line up with our ration books for meat. This was provided in the local village butcher shop, about three miles from the farm.

I don't remember exactly how we were allowed to keep poultry, but it must have been legal, or the official from the department of Agriculture would have found out, since all the cottages kept chickens, plus a few ducks and geese. So we had eggs, and we ate either a goose or a fat chicken or two, sharing them with our good friends the neighbours on special celebrations and at Christmas time.

On such occasions, all the cottage doors were open to welcome you in, share a glass of homemade, wine or beer for the adults, and homemade stone ginger pop for the kids, and all guests were expected to sit and eat with the family.

Once a fortnight Cyril and I would join the other farm kids to sit on the top of a grassy bank, to watch the provisions van labouring up the hill to the farm. The attraction was oranges as they were the big attraction; we had not seen a orange or banana in many a month, and were ever hopeful that the Grocery man would have a few on this visit. I don't know what make of van it was or even the colour, but I remember it was tall and long. (Everything was 'tall and long' to me in those days!)

As the men were out in the fields working, it meant only the wives and kids fresh back from school were surrounding the van in expectancy of that rear door opening, the counter gently brought down into place on the hinge, and the fat grocer man with the red face, booming out his jovial spiel; 'Now then ladies, have I got something good for you today. Bananas! Yes, and a few oranges too. Just arrived at Glasgow docks, and I know they are fresh, because I've just been and picked them up right from the ship with my own fair hands!' The women would giggle and tell the grinning grocer what a fibber he was.

That provisions van was a Pandora's Box to us kids. We wanted to see inside, but it was so high off the ground that all we could ever see was the fat grocer in his brown overall leaning on the counter chatting up our mums. We tried to imagine what lay within those magical walls; for there was an overall concoction of smells from paraffin to candles, mixed in with the strong smell of accumulator battery acid and beeswax; disinfectant, fire lighters, and other aromas we could not identify.

A few miscellaneous items such as broom heads, wooden spade handles, stoves, coal shovels, all placed neatly in the racks on the side of the van, or piled into two shiny new metal dustbins near the rear door. The grocer would continue with his banter;

"As I say, I have a special today ladies. Lovely Jaffa oranges, or a few bananas, and I've saved them just for you. Only two coupons and two bob for two oranges or two bananas." Two 'bob' was a Slang word in those days for two shillings, a lot of money to spend on what was nothing more than luxuries.

I do not know if he was a good salesperson, but in such circumstances when exotic fruit or any other scarce item was available to him, he could soon do brisk business. In the end, most mothers bought one large orange or two bananas, after bartering with the grocer to reduce the asking price. Later the fruit would be carefully cut into equal pieces for each member of the family to enjoy a morsel of the tropical fruit.

Often the woman would do a little un-official business bartering with him to get something they knew he kept hidden under the counter. The mums would magically produce a much sought after portion of home cured ham that had been hanging for months (before ration books came in) from hooks in the kitchen ceiling, or a couple of freshly killed chickens; in exchange for 200 cigarettes, or a bottle of whisky or brandy.

As the months of the war rolled on and the Navy began to beat the U-boat packs, more supply ships arrived in British ports, and hitherto scarce items became more readily available, and the Grocery Van had more to offer.

8. *'Far Eastern Delights'*

On one trip to Hong Kong, I recall going ashore and making a bee-line for the Hong Kong Fleet Club, since we were allowed all night furlough, and one of the joys of staying at the club was a clean, comfortable bed with fresh sheets. A refreshing break from the 24 hours a day noise from dynamos and other working machines below deck on the ship, and certainly much better food in the canteen. We were allowed to wear civilian clothes once we had checked into the Club, as Hong Kong was still a British Colony at that period of time, but we had to change back into our uniforms before returning aboard ship for duty the next morning.

I remember that I went swimming in the club pool, had a few beers and a good meal in the canteen, and then decided I would have an early night, and went to bed. Although I had a small travel alarm clock, I phoned through to the reception desk and booked a wake-up call just to be sure I woke up on time. I had to be back on board my ship at 7.30am, so I could get ready for the first duty of the day, when the band was required to play for morning parade of raising the colours ceremony.

I awoke about 6am, and dressed in my uniform and walked back to the ship, which only took me about 20 minutes. As I approached the gangway, a man was standing almost naked with only a bath towel around his middle, and asked me if my name was Weddell. I replied that it was, and cheekily asked why he wanted to know.

He was a Naval Officer that I had not recognized, for we only saw them now and then, when the band was required to play ceremonial music. He gave me a telling off 'for being insubordinate' and identified himself as an officer and told me to report immediately to the officer's Wardroom, as a detective from the Hong Kong Police was waiting to question me!

On arriving at the Officer's Wardroom door, a mess steward met me and told me to wait in the passageway. The door slid open, and a tall European man dressed in full Hong Kong Police uniform smiled at me, and asked where I had been last night?

I had nothing to hide, and told him about the Hong Kong Fleet Club, producing the stub of my booking ticket. He was satisfied, and explained that a man of my size wearing a Marine uniform had assaulted a rickshaw driver who was now in hospital with broken ribs and facial injuries.

We were in Hong Kong for six days after completing sea exercises with warships from several nations, and as young men will do after several weeks at sea, a Marine from one of the American ships had got into a rickshaw and asked the driver to take him to a 'house of ill repute' (brothel) and to wait for him.

When the Marine came out, he asked the rickshaw driver to take him to a bar on the waterfront, and then the trouble started when the rickshaw driver demanded a ridiculously high fare in advance.

Rickshaw drivers are very fit, from peddling passengers in the cycle rickshaw; the marine refused to pay him at all, and started walking away, and a fight started. The marine pushed the driver over, and he fell backwards, banging his head on the cobbled stones, and not content with this, the marine had put the boot in and kicked the unfortunate Chinese man several times, as he lay on the ground and then ran off to join his friends in one of the many bars on the waterfront.

Other rickshaw drivers had come to the aid of the poor chap that had been injured, but not quick enough to catch up with the marine who was running away, and did not see which bar he had entered. He was reported to be 'very tall' and that is why I was being questioned, because a couple of rickshaw drivers had seen me walking back to my ship early in the morning. We sailed before we heard any further news of what happened; either to the marine, or to the recovery of the rickshaw man. So being tall does not always have its advantages.

Part of our duties included visits aboard HMS Alert to other Countries in the Far East, and on one such occasion we visited the Philippines, to the large Capital city of Manila.

The Senior Officer of the Manila Police band, much to our surprise, greeted us when we docked, and invited us all to visit the Police barracks for lunch. A bus was laid on and transported all 20 of us to the depot and we were taken straight into their mess hall and treated to a fine traditional local meal, but I cannot really recall what the dish was, except that it was good. That much I can remember.

After lunch we were invited to listen to the Police band in rehearsal, and entering a very large auditorium we were surprised and delighted to see a huge concert band sat ready to play. We discovered later that there were 120 musicians sitting there - and boy did they make a good noise!

The first piece of music was Tchaikovsky's 1812 Overture, and it was superb, for we sat there with the hairs on the back of our necks raised! It was a real thrill to hear such a good band. They played several other pieces for us and then the conductor turned around and invited our Band Officer to take the baton, and conduct the band.

It was obvious to us that they did not want to embarrass their guest conductor by playing something he would not have seen before, so they gave him a march that all bands play, "The Stars and Stripes Forever' by John Philip Sousa. It was magnificent, and we sat there very proud of our boss, for he did a splendid job of conducting those fine musicians.

After the concert was over, the band came around us and started talking about music, and their boss asked our boss if we could come back with our instruments and perform for them.

So later in the evening we did, for our Admiral had gone to a dinner party ashore, and did not require our services, and the Captain of HMS Alert gave us permission to return to the Police barracks that evening.

There was no way just 20 of us could possibly out match such a fine band as they had, but our boss was smart, and told the Police Chief we would perform our parade ceremony of 'Beating the Retreat,' a ritual that goes back many decades in the British Royal Navy.

We turned up at the barracks in our ceremonial dress uniforms, and they switched on the parade ground flood lights, and we began our show for the police band and a couple of hundred guests that had magically appeared, no doubt hearing about it on the 'internal grapevine'.

We were pretty good at doing this parade ceremony, for we had done it hundreds of times in our service with the Royal Marines. Everything went faultless from start to finish with no split notes from either the band or the bugler's that played the 'Last Post' at the end of the display, and the crowd went mad!

The Police Band Chief came over to our boss at the end of the display when we had marched off the parade ground, and was shaking his hand up and down and really ecstatic about the 'wonderful British tradition' of ceremonial parades.

There was no way any of us in that band were anywhere near the standard of musicianship of his players, but we were just good at parade stuff and that really counted that evening. Needless to say, that we left that place a little wobbly after all the beer the Police band poured down our throats after the parade.

That was not the end of our delightful trip to the Philippines, because the very next day our band was invited to perform at a garden party held in the gardens of the Managing Director of the Becks Brewery franchise in Manila. His house, or rather the property of Becks, was almost next to the brewery, so that was handy not just for him, but for us too, because after we played for about fifty minutes, the MD came over and invited us all into the brewery, and gave us a quick tour, followed by a 'quick taster' as he called it, downing lots of bottles of cold beer from their special line called Bok, and it was not only delicious, but also very potent, and our Officer had to call 'time' and get us back aboard the bus, for return to the ship before we got even more drunk.

Life for the Royal Marine Band at that time in HMS Terror was more like a paid extended holiday, for we did not really have many duties to do after the morning parade had finished. At nine thirty, we would go down to the band storage room and bring out the music stands and music, and putting it all onto a porter's trolley, we lugged it up the hill to the mess hall (dining rooms) and set up for band practice.

This would be two or three times a week, and we packed up at midday, as the mess hall had to be prepared for lunch at 12 noon to 1pm. Afternoons were free for us to do as we pleased, when we were not required to travel to a parade in another part of Singapore, or perform in the evening for the Officer's dinner parties, or for the Admiral.

Our trips to Hong Kong were numerous. As I have mentioned before hand, we invariably travelled aboard HMS Alert, the flagship of the Admiral of the British Far East fleet, but now and then, we would fly by RAF plane, but that was not very often. The Admiral's ship had a quarterdeck the size of a cruiser, for this is where all the cocktail parties were held, under a striped canvas awning in sunny weather. For those of you that do not know what a quarterdeck is, this is an open space of wooden decking on the rear of the vessel.

The wooden covered quarter deck on the 'Alert' was scrubbed white by the sailors, and only the Marine Band and officers on duty, were allowed to enter that hallowed area.

One memorable trip was taken to the land of the rising Sun, Japan. It was to be the first official visit of a British Warship since before the Second World War. We entered the Inland Sea during the early hours of the morning, and made our way up to the (then) small town named Wakayama, and anchored in the bay.

In these modern times the city of Wakayama, which is well known as the castle town of the Kishu branch of Gosanke, (the three successor houses of Tokugawa), is located at the mouth of the Kino-Kawa River, and is blessed with a mild climate and an abundance of greenery. There is also Wakayama Marina City which holds an amusement park, and with the construction of hotels and apartments, the city has become attractive (to those that can afford it) as a resort for long term residence. The opening of Kansai International Airport has made the city easy to access from outside the prefecture.

When we awoke in the morning, there was a mist over the water, and we assembled on the quarterdeck in our ceremonial uniforms and awaited the arrival of our hosts, the local dignitaries. The ship was dressed from the top mast to the deck in colourful bunting, and everyone looked extremely smart. The Admiral of the British Far East Fleet stood to attention alongside the Captain of HMS Alert as the Japanese naval motor boats came alongside our ship, and the Japanese dignitaries stepped onto the scrubbed white woodwork of the gangplank and up to the deck, being piped aboard by the traditional naval bosun's whistle. The British Ambassador to Japan, who accompanied the local officials, introduced our Admiral to the leading Japanese Dignitary, the Mayor of Wakayama, who was dressed in a long tailed morning suit and top hat, looking as if he had stepped out of an old photograph from the days of Queen Victoria. (I apologise to anyone of Japanese decent that may be reading this book as no offence is intended; it was just the way these Gentlemen were dressed in those far off days.)

There was much bowing before the Mayor and his colleagues were ushered down to the Admiral's stateroom for official document exchanges, and no doubt a drink of some sort. The whole ceremony took about 45 minutes, and during this time we had to play music and remain standing to attention with the rest of the ship's company. This is not easy to do, and you can get cramp, if you do not move your toes gently inside your boots. One of the sailors fainted, and was quickly removed from the area and taken to sick bay. We heard later that he had been put on a charge for not eating breakfast, which caused him to faint in the first place. His punishment was pulling an extra duty on board, and not being allowed ashore for the few hours we were in port, and that must have been hard on him as the rest of his mates and the band had the freedom of the town. Wakayama was charming, with beautiful miniature gardens full of flowers and bushes, waterfalls, and ornamental curved bridges crossing over ponds filled with colourful fish. Unfortunately, I did not own a camera in those days, so no pictures are available.

Women still wore the traditional kimono dress with white socks and sandals, although there were a few that wore western clothes. Some local men wore trilby hats and suits, and hurried around the streets bowing to us foreigners in our uniform, and in return, we bowed back.

Wakayama was only a small town at that time and it did not take long to see everything, and we all soon returned to the ship for the evening meal.

Then we set sail for Tokyo; it was only a one day visit and not enough time to really see the city; but we went into the Ginza at that time, the main street, and which today has grown into a whole district that tourists love to visit because English is spoken in most of the large department stores and restaurants.

We wanted to try a Japanese meal and taste their beer. There was no interest in Saki rice wine, because we could easily get that back in Singapore; and we found lots of fancy restaurants, but our meagre amount of money would not run to the prices on the menu we saw in the windows, so we decided on a workman's café instead. Even there the prices were high, and we ended up just having one small beer since it was so expensive, and returned to the ship very hungry lads ready to devour the evening meal.

I cannot remember much more about the Tokyo visit, except that we did do a band concert in a park to a large audience, of mostly school children, who seemed to enjoy listening to our music. I do recall having to play a trombone solo out front of the band entitled 'Loves Enchantment' written by Arthur Pryor, a gifted American trombonist from the early part of the Century.

Anyone who has played this piece will tell you it is no walk over, and needs lots of practise and care to develop the skills to play it with confidence.

But we were glad to get back on board the ship and returning to Singapore via Hong Kong, for it was like a second home port to us. The Admiral always seemed to have lots of official duties there, and we had to play music for his engagements and that meant freedom for a few hours afterwards in a much less expensive city than Tokyo.

Quite often we would be called to play in the British Consul for special occasions, such as 'Beating the retreat'. This would always be a boozy affair, as the Consul would lavish crates of beer on the members of the band, much to the dismay of our Bandmaster, but we behaved ourselves and did not let him down.

On another occasion, we made a visit to Rangoon in Burma. It was to play music at the British residency, and only the band was involved, apart from a few sailors off HMS Alert, to act as waiters at the garden party reception in the grounds.

We sat on the edge of the large lawn area in the shade of a light covering of pink and white striped awning, performing a medley of British songs, such as 'In an English Country Garden' and Henry Wood's sea songs and shanties; 'We'll keep a welcome in the hillside' 'On Mother Kelly's doorstep' 'Bluebells of Scotland' and 'There will always be an England' ending with 'Rule Britannia.' This was a standard choice of music to play in foreign lands to promote the United Kingdom, but quite possibly, without intention of course, making quite a few expat Brits stationed abroad, feel really homesick!

I recall that the residency staff decided to put us up in a nearby annex which was a potting shed of some sort, and we discovered some rustling noises in a corner behind some boxes, and one of the band members kicked a box and a black snake slid out from behind it, rapidly vanishing into the bushes outside the door.

We even received a visit from the Ambassador's wife herself, to ensure we were being looked after properly. She apologised profusely for not being able to supply us with beer, as it was a difficult British product to obtain in Burma at that time, and hoped we would not mind sharing a dozen bottles of chilled Bollinger Champagne?

Talking about free booze at events that we performed in ashore in foreign parts, there was the time we arrived in Saigon. It was only a short visit, but the French were fighting a war with the Communists pushing down through the jungles of North Vietnam into South Vietnam even then, prior to the Americans becoming involved, but Saigon was still firmly in the hands of the French and safe at the time of our official visit.

I recall the wide Parisian style streets with the sidewalk cafes, and even today I can see in my mind's eye, the rows of trees lining the pavements.

We were invited to play in the French Army Barracks, and after the parade, we sat in a stand inside a large arena and watched a show of beautiful horses doing wonderful moves and dancing. Then the French invited us to lunch, and as most people know, they like to drink wine when they eat.

Us lot in the Marine Band were not used to this, and when liberal amounts of red table wine were placed in large Carafe's on the tables it was soon consumed by us all, and within half an hour we were all on the way to being drunk before the Band Sergeant spotted it, and told the French not to serve any more wine. Spoilsport!

This was when I reported sick to the Medical centre (sick bay) on board the ship the next morning as I had lost vision in my left eye. There was no Doctor on board HMS Alert, only when the Admiral was on board, so I was sent to the French Army Hospital for treatment. This is covered elsewhere in these stories, so no need to go over it again.

9. *'Meanwhile, back on the farm…'*

I recall clearly the time when Uncle George came back to the farm. He was in the Argyle and Southern Highlanders regiment and had been granted seven days leave.

He was always good to us boys, and one Saturday afternoon he had taken my mum and dad and sister to Edinburgh on the bus, to do some shopping. Cyril and I had been left in the care of a neighbour, whose kids we were always playing with, so it was fine by us.

When they eventually rolled back home around ten at night, they were singing their heads off as they walked into our neighbour's house, for a few visits to the local pubs on the way home had capped their great day out for them. Seeing us two lads, Uncle George called us over and ruffled our heads with his rough hands.

"I've a wee present for ye both." With a big smile on his face, he told us to follow him to our house. "Now Cyril, I ken ye was wantin' a bike, so here you are laddie!" He opened the wood storage hut door and there stood a gleaming new 'Hopper' bike.

Cyril's face lit up as he said 'Cor, look Leslie –it's got five gears on it!' I could see my brother was impressed, even though I had feelings of being left out. He gave Uncle a big hug and said "Thanks Uncle, its great!'

Uncle George had a twinkle in his eyes when he turned to me and said "Go in the house, Leslie, and you will find a present waiting for you." I really wanted that bike. But I loved my brother and was happy for him. With mixed feelings I slunk into the house and looked around. I could not see anything out of the ordinary in the room.

"Look in your bedroom, laddie!" Uncle George roared.

Entering the bedroom I saw a small cardboard box in the corner. George had followed me in with my mum and dad close behind. "Open the box, Jim, your present is inside!" Not knowing what to expect, I opened the box with trepidation, and out popped the little head of a Collie sheepdog.

" Eeoow!" I cried, "A puppy dog!" I was suddenly on cloud nine.

"Do you like him?" Mum asked.

I had picked the dog up and was holding him close to me and he was licking my face. "Oh yes, he is lovely!" I said happily, and thanked Uncle George for his generosity.

Mum gently patted me on my back and said "Leslie, now remember, you have to look after him properly because everyone else is too busy, and he is now your dog, and you must take him for walks and feed him and wash him too, as well as clean up after him until he is house trained."

I was so happy to do all these things without question because I always wanted a dog of my own. There were several dogs on the farm, but none of them were mine. They were working dogs that the farmer used to gather in the sheep and cattle. Now I had my very own, and I was in heaven.

"What are you going to call him?" Dad asked.

"Jed!" I exclaimed.

"Oh yes, a great name for a male dog!" Mum said with a big smile, for she could see I was so happy. Cyril was delighted too, for he loved dogs, and we decided in bed that night, that we would share the bike and Jed between us.

To get to school, Cyril and I joined the other four farm children to walk together across five fields. I distinctly remember the number, because we did that journey every day of every term, for at least three years. I can't remember how long it took, but it must have been around half an hour, in good weather.

With the inquisitive nature that all children have, we explored the hedges for bird nests and small animals, often finding a lonely hedgehog and prodding it gently with a twig to see it roll up into a ball. We knew the names of most of the species of wild birds that inhabit that region, and of course rabbits, hares, field mice and voles, moles, weasels, fox and badger.

We gathered leaves from the ground in autumn on our way to school, and would then trace, or press, them onto paper in our art class sessions. In summer, we ate our way to school and back with all the wild raspberries, blackberries, and gooseberries we could find. During these nature feasts we would often get stung by nettles when we climbed through them to get at the berries, but that was not a problem either, for we had the time honoured country folk cure for the sting, by rubbing dock leaves over the inflamed parts to bring relief.

In December through to late February, we often had a heavy snowfall; but this rarely deterred us sturdy country children from attending school, no matter how deep the snow drifts were that we had to climb through to reach the warm classrooms.

As Jed grew larger he followed us everywhere, even to school. We could often see him through our classroom window, lying on the grass with a grin on his face as his tongue lolled from the side of his mouth.

At break times the caretaker would take him a bowl of water, and now and then give him a biscuit or a chunk of his lunch sandwich, even though we pleaded with him not to, for Jed was going to be trained as a working sheep dog. Well, that was my plan anyway. It was only when he was about six months old that we realized he had a limp in one of his back legs, and asked the farmer what we should do, for he had three working sheep dogs and was experienced in these things.

"Aye, he's limping alright. Ye better bring him in the mornin' when the vet is due to see my cows for cleansing. But mind this. He is a busy man, so don't be botherin' him whilst he works!"

The vet did examine Jed, and told us he was born with a weakness in his left hind leg and that he would never be strong enough to be anything other than our house pet. So that was that. Jed did not seem to mind, for he was always bounding about and barking, with that silly grin on his face as though he was laughing at you.

When he was in the mood, he would often sit quietly next to Dad whilst he was reading his paper, and after a while he would put a paw on father's leg to indicate he wanted to go for a walk. Dad always went for a walk with Mum in the nice evenings, and Jed was good company running around them and stopping here and there to sniff something, or urinating to leave his scent on the base of a tree, or a bush.

Every night he would sneak into our bedroom and lie quietly on the floor, until mother popped her head round the door to see if we were asleep, then she would point at Jed sternly with her finger, and he would get up and sleek out of our room on his haunches, and into the hallway to his basket. In the summer months he lived outside at nights, sleeping contentedly in the woodshed with the door ajar.

On a late sunny afternoon in April of 1944, a truck pulled up outside the farmhouse and out of it jumped six men. They could not have been more than eighteen or twenty years of age and were all dressed in the same new working clothes, and wearing shiny new boots. Having just returned from school, my brother and I joined the other children and collectively made our way up to the farmhouse, curious to find out whom these new people were.

One of them smiled at us and said "Bambinos!" His friends turned, and with huge smiles on their faces, waved at us all. The farmer was talking to the driver of the truck, and when he finished, he spoke briefly to us children.

"Boys and Girls, these lads are Italian prisoners of war, and they will be living with us for a few weeks, to help with the harvest. They do not speak much English, so I don't want you pestering them, you hear? Be nice – and don't call them names!"

They were soon billeted in the spare cottage in the middle of the row of six, and the neighbours all went indoors, no doubt suspicious of POW's coming to work on the farm. After all, they were foreigners, and were our enemy. Two days went by without even a murmur from the Italians, who must have felt the tension from the neighbours, and simply appeared at 6am each morning in the main farmyard for the farmer to allocate work duties to them.

The POW's were hard workers and did their work well without supervision, and were always singing in the fields, in the cow barn when mucking out, or in their cottage after work. They smiled at everyone and said in broken English "Gud Morning, itsa greata day!" or words to that effect.

Then, within the week they came knocking on all the doors, washed and smartly dressed in the new civilian clothes they had been given. In broken English, one of them explained that they were all farm workers back in Italy before being conscripted by Mussolini's henchmen and forced into the army.

The Italians were going to have a party on the following Saturday in their cottage and wanted everyone to come, and on the appointed day it was a fine evening and they welcomed the few neighbours who had bothered to come. I am pleased to say that the entire Weddell family, including Uncle George, who had been demobbed by this time because he had returned to his former essential job as a coal miner, was present.

That was our first introduction to pasta, and several other Italian dishes. They were good cooks, and the house was spotlessly clean. Communication was a problem at first, as everyone was trying to stutter out a few words in broken English or Italian, the latter mostly from Uncle George, who fancied himself as an interpreter. I suspect the Italian lads didn't have a clue what he was trying to say most of the time, and just smiled and 'bello, bello, bello-ed' a lot. Trying to learn to speak English from a bunch of Scottish folks is hard enough for any foreigner, but those Italian lads did their best.

Having only arrived on the farm and still trustee POW's, they were not allowed to go off the property for any reason, and had to muster twice a day at the Farm House to ensure there were no absentees. So they apologised for not having any 'Vino,' and that was soon understood, and bottles of homemade wine from neighbours soon appeared, much to their joy, for they had not had any alcohol since being taken prisoners.

In retrospect, I don't think the farmer or the military would have been impressed with this blatant breach of the rules. But, since Mr Cummings never came down to the cottages, and his large farmhouse was almost a quarter of a mile down the road, nobody was going to know about the party.

The young Italians were gentlemen and behaved themselves, and as more wine was consumed the singing got louder, and we all danced around in the back garden, for by now everyone in the cottages had turned up to join the fiesta.

As the party got into full swing, more food magically appeared from houses, carried in by the women, and the Italians were aghast with surprise at the generosity of their new neighbours, when they saw the cured hams and home churned cheeses being placed on the table.

"Mamma Mia!" cried one of the goggled eyed lads who had dropped to his knees, clasping his hands. He began to cry, and Mrs McGregor put her arm around his shoulder and said, "Poor wee bairin, I reckon he's missin' his Ma!" she exclaimed. That party was the first of many to come, and they got better when one of the Italians was given an old accordion by my Uncle George. It was a bit out of tune, and several of the ivory keys were missing, but the lad fixed it up and turned out to be a fair musician on the instrument. We had many traditional Italian and Sicilian songs and dances, and he even learned to play a few Scottish reels by listening and learning to play them from the radio.

The door to their kitchen was always open and anyone was welcome in, always with a genuine smile and a cup of tea and a home baked scone or biscuit, Italian style of course. Then there were the washing lines hanging in the sitting room. Instead of clothes, their homemade pasta was hanging up to dry!

We had marvellous parties after work in the summer; all sitting in the garden with coloured lighting rigged up now that the war had come to an end.

The POW's were there on the farm for nearly three months, and never in all that time, did they say a cross word, or did anything to upset anyone. They were eventually taken away by truck to be repatriated back to their homeland, and for many years afterwards, we used to remember those wonderful and happy days, when the Italians lived with us all on the farm.

It was early on a Sunday morning when a car drew up outside our cottage and a man and a woman got out, and knocked on our door. Still in bed, and sleepy eyed, my brother and I just turned over to go back to the land of nod, when we heard loud arguing between Mum and the female stranger. Both of us got up, went into the living room, and looked through the window. The strangers were getting back into the car, and the woman was shouting at my mother. "I'll be back with the police! You are not keeping them!"

Neither of us understood that statement, but we both had a strange feeling that something was very wrong, and went to ask Mum. She was crying, and Dad was trying to console her. She grabbed both of us boys and held us close to her. "She is not getting them back after all this time –it's not fair!"

Well, it happened. It was not until the following day, but on that fateful Monday, mother came to school at lunch time to bring us both home early. We had to get dressed up in our best suits, and went with her and Dad to the town of Haddington, in which the courts were situated in the Lothian Counties at that time. We sat in the waiting room nervously looking around, and wondering what was going on, for our parents had still not given us an explanation. Mum was constantly hugging both of us and dabbing her eyes with a handkerchief.

Then I noticed the two strangers sitting at the other side of the waiting room. The man just looked straight ahead but the woman kept glaring at our mum, and smiling at us. I tugged on his sleeve and asked my Father, why is that woman staring at us? "You will see in a minute, son." He replied hoarsely.

The door in the middle of the room opened, and a woman came in. "Would both parties, please come in?" A man dressed in a dark suit sat at a table facing us. He was studying the papers on the desk in front of him. After what seemed an eternity to all of us, he lifted his head, removed his spectacles, and spoke. Neither Cyril nor I understood what he was talking about, except that it seemed to make my mother cry, and say, "It's not fair, we have looked after them since they were babies!"

Even at that young age, I had a bad feeling that something serious was about to happen to our lives. I was not wrong, for two women appeared wearing some sort of uniform, and came over and asked Cyril to go with them.

He began crying and shouting "Mum! Where are they taking me? Dad, help me! Leslie, please help me –why are they taking me away?" It was heartbreaking, because I tried to get up from my seat to go to my brother, but Dad firmly held me down, and I could see he had a tear in his eyes too, for he was trying to console my mother, who was wailing in despair and shouting for Cyril. The strangers stood up, and without saying a word, followed the women taking my brother Cyril away through that door.

I never saw him again.

When we returned to the farm my parents tried to explain to me and my sister why Cyril had been taken away from us. Before coming to live on the farm, both John and Jean Weddell had lived in Craigmiller, a district in Edinburgh. He was working at the Theatre Royal as a stage technician, and Jean worked in a café as the cook. In those days, many people lived in poverty and cramped conditions, and Craigmiller was a new estate to try and relieve some of this misery.

Because Mr & Mrs Weddell had jobs and a young child (Jeanette), they were lucky to be given an apartment in the new estate. Getting to know many of the other tenants, they befriended the Addis family. They had six children, including two baby boys, and neither parent had a job, and depended on small handouts from the Salvation Army and the other charity organizations. Back then, there was no social welfare blanket system like there is today, in Britain.

The State decided the Addis Parents just could not care for six children, and were asked to find foster homes for the babies. So the family agreed to let the Weddell family take Cyril and myself, and foster us until such time as the Addis's were able to satisfy the state that they could take us back, and bring us up properly.

On that fateful day Cyril was torn from us in the Fiscal office, it had been agreed that only one boy should be returned to the original parents, and as Cyril was the youngest, he was chosen. Why there was never any visitation agreement made I will never know, but we tried everything to find the Addis family and my dear brother Cyril, all to no avail, for the court would not reveal their address, and we could not find them, even though we tried every means available to us at that time.

We visited Craigmiller, but they had long moved away from there, and the housing office had no records as to a forwarding address, as the Addis's had left owing a month rent. It took a very long time to adjust to my new life without my brother. It felt like he had died, and in reality it was much the same thing, as I would never see him again.

Life on the farm went on for another year, and my only real friend was trusty old Jed. He seemed to know Cyril was not coming back,and he slept on the bed were Cyril used to sleep, and never left my side for weeks on end, following me more than ever before. In the first weeks after my brother was taken away from us, Jed was constantly with his paws up on the window sill, looking in the hope that Cyril would suddenly appear once again.

Uncle George had gone back to his coal mining job at Lonehead pit and lived in a small apartment free of rent provided by the company. Jeanette had got married and moved into a council house with her new husband in a small village near Edinburgh, leaving just the three of us on the farm. Then in late 1946 more tragedy struck the family when my Father took ill, and was admitted to the Edinburgh Royal Infirmary.

He never came back to the farm again. He died from lung Cancer within a month, and heartbroken, my mother took me south to live in England, with her sister in Walsall, in the Midlands, where she had been born.

I have always looked upon John and Jean Weddell as my proper parents. They looked after Cyril and myself and loved us, and to me they will always be Mum and Dad. I have tried several times over the years to contact my brother, but have never succeeded.

And Jed? We gave him to the Farmer, since he spent most of his time running around with the other dogs, and he was far better off staying there than leaving the freedom of a farm to live in any town.

10. 'Goodbye, Scotland, Hello England'

Being uprooted from a quiet Scottish farm and suddenly finding myself in a drab, noisy town, took a bit of getting used to. In the heart of the midlands of England, Walsall is one of the many towns in the sprawling hub around the city of Birmingham.

Back in the 1950's most of the heavy engineering plants and foundries of Britain were situated in those towns, and Walsall was one of them. With its large labour force of skilled workers being employed by the huge F.H. Lloyds steel works in Darleston, a suburb of Walsall. Known to traditionalists as the 'Black Country' where the coal seam comes to the surface - West Bromwich, Oldbury, Blackheath, Cradley Heath, Old Hill, Bilston, Dudley, Tipton, Wednesfield and parts of Halesowen, Wednesbury and Walsall.

The massive steel works turned out everything from strip steel sheeting, to finished boiler components. I recall standing with my mother in a small crowd one day, watching a group of workers trying to get a huge trailer truck with its massive load, through the narrow gates of the old factory.

After a good hour of head scratching and measuring the width of the load, the bosses must have come to the conclusion that the only way to get the vehicle clear of the premises was to remove the gates, and then having to knock down five feet or so of brickwork on either side, to get the massive load out onto the street.

It was quite a spectacle, and a decent sized crowd had gathered on the opposite side of the street to watch the operation. I had never seen anything so big in my young life before this. By the looks of it, it was part of a ship's boiler.

The red lead painted bulk was secured by thick chains onto the middle of a long, low bogey trailer, with more wheels on it than I could count. It was so long that there was an extra driving cab fixed on the tail end of the trailer to aid steering. It must have taken them about two and a half hours in all to get that thing rolling out into the street, before it set off at a very slow pace with a police escort, creeping along with bright warning lights flashing, in front and rear of the juggernaut to clear the way through the traffic.

In the early 1950's, along with most of the industrial towns of England, Walsall was still a dreary place with terrace houses and narrow cobbled streets. Even on sunny days the whole place looked bleak and forbidding, due to the years of belching coal smoke from hundreds of tall chimneys coating everything in thick, black grime.

I was still grieving for my brother Cyril, and the wonderful life I had known on the farm. I just could not take it in, why my Mother had decided we had to leave that wonderful place of tranquillity, for this dump. I had always been a free mind, and to me, no longer being able to romp in the fields with my brother and the other children we grew up with, was incomprehensible. I did not understand that when my Father passed away, we had to leave the farm, as he would be replaced by a new man that would be living in 'our' cottage with his family.

To add to my misery, I could not adjust to my Aunty, the strange woman who was my Mother's sister, with whom we were lodged. She had been married to a man named Norman Whittaker, who worked in the local steel mills until his premature death in an accident at work. 'Auntie Margaret' had received a considerable sum of money in compensation for the loss of her husband, and had bought a fancy semi detached three bedroom house with the proceeds, in what the locals would consider a posh part of town, filling it with expensive furniture and luxuries.

Mum had warned me that 'Auntie Margaret' had no children of her own, and was a bit strange; so I really had to be as quiet as a mouse, and on my very best behaviour whilst we lived there. It would only be for a short while, for she was quickly going to find work, and look for a place of our own.

It could not come fast enough for me.

The second our eyes met, I instinctively knew that Aunty Margeret disliked me. Oh, she was nice as pie, but I could detect the coldness in her stare when she shook my hand. When you are just eleven years old, you can't possibly understand why some adults do not like children. I felt awful. I was on the point of tears, and desperately wanted at that moment to get right back on the train to Edinburgh. Everything seemed like a bad dream. At any moment I expected to wake up and find myself safely in bed, back on the farm with Cyril and Dad, and even my sister Jeanette.

I had never seen wall-to-wall carpets on a floor before, nor fancy curtains and large sofas, and there was something called central heating in the house too. The stair walls were lined with those insipid mock porcelain flying ducks, so popular in the forties and fifties, and the first thing I managed to do was, knock one of them off the wall as I clumsily made my way up the stairs, dragging a large suitcase behind me.

Margaret was at the top of the stairs leading the way to our bedroom, and on hearing the crash, she turned and glared at me. Mum said "For goodness sakes Leslie - be more careful!" She turned and apologized to her sister, who said nothing, but tight lipped, she continued up the stairs.

For the next ten days, I had to remain in that house, not venturing further than the front garden, in fear of getting lost. Auntie Margaret fed me, but scrimpingly, when my mother was out in the town, searching for work.

Mercifully, she found a job within a few days, in a busy café in the town centre, and was soon installed as one of the cooks. The owner told her of a house that was for rent, and we moved out of Aunty Margaret's rooms by the end of the week.

I never saw her again, and was vastly relieved to be away from her stingy food helpings and stringent rules about 'You can't sit there! You can't do that! Get up the stairs to the room!" whilst my mother was out, and I was left in her charge.

We must have lived in our 'new' house for six or seven years. It was in a suburb of Walsall called Palfrey, and was a Victorian style two up and two down dwelling. The toilet was in the back yard, but thankfully close to the house, and not at the end of a long garden, like on the farm back in Scotland.

I attended a local school until I was about thirteen, and Mother decided to send me to a Boy's school run by the Shaftsbury Homes trust. As I said before, I was a bit of a free spirit, and was now becoming a tear away, spending too much time out of the house after school with other boys of questionable character, whilst my mother worked the long hours in the café. She had applied for a bursary for me to attend Fortesque House School in Twickenham, Middlesex, approximately twenty miles outside of the city of London.

My new school was a noble looking large country style house that once belonged to Lord Fortesque, situated behind a high brick wall running the length of the property, with large leafy chestnut trees, and a mixture of crab apple bushes and assorted fauna in the grounds.

Behind the building, a large, well-kept lawn separated the playground and classrooms from the dormitories. It was a peaceful and tranquil setting, and I liked the look of the place as soon as we spotted it on our short walk from the Strawberry Hill railway station. I lugged my suitcase up the avenue through the beautiful arc of popular trees, with a sense of excitement running through me. Mother was talking all the way, assuring me I would soon settle down and enjoy my new school. I could come home for visits, as they allowed children in those days to travel alone.

The Headmaster was Dr. Leslie Pierce, and he greeted us warmly, when we were shown into his study. He wore the traditional teacher's black gown, and rose from his seat to greet us, placing a huge pipe in the ashtray as he did so. "Mrs. Weddell, how nice to meet you!" He shook her hand, and turned to me. "Ah, you must be young Leslie, the boy I have heard so much about." He shook my hand too. Nobody had shaken my hand before; perhaps my neck, as Dad used to do playfully, when I was tormenting him.

It turned out I really did like Fortesque House, because I lived and learned in that establishment until I reached my sixteenth birthday. I never was much good at math, or even English, and I certainly did not have a clue about learning French, which I found exceedingly boring. However, I did like music, and that turned out to be my forte.

Because of my thick Scottish accent, all the children, and even some of the more amiable teachers, addressed me as 'Jock'. It did not bother me and I had that handle for many years, until my accent started to gradually diminish, as I became older.

Before arriving at Fortesque House School, I had no inclination to want to play music, although I did enjoy listening to the radio with my family, and would join in singing a song if I knew the words.

My first introduction to music at the school came from a friend who was in the school band that played the Cornet. "You will like it Jock, for bandmaster Rask, is a great guy, and will teach you how to play an instrument." I went with Ron to listen to the band. The band room was next to the school medical centre, which sounds grand, but in reality, was a spare recreation room annex in the hospital.

A visiting Doctor would examine children on his weekly visits. For all other minor ailments, we had nurse Williams, a rather plump, and pleasant, lady who always wore a large starched white headdress over a blue uniform, which was the way the nursing profession looked in the early fifties.

Mr. Rask was busy doing something to the valves of a cornet, and talking to the boy concerned about the need for regular attention to his instrument. I sat at the back of the room in the bay window, where there was a wooden stool. There must have been about twenty lads all sat there with instruments, all blowing away and making a noise.

"QUIET!" roared Mr Rask. 'You are making so much noise I can't hear myself think!' He beamed as they all finally stopped the dreadful din. "Let's start with a march. Colonel Bogey is a good one, and we've been working on it for a few weeks now, so it should sound at least half decent!"

Ron, my Cornet playing friend, half turned and gave me a wink. Mr. Rask counted them in, and they started playing. To my ears, it sounded no different from the din they were all making individually, when the boss was fixing the valves. He waved his hands around in the air and shouted for them to stop. With a look of disgust on his face, he announced, "Boys, you sound like a bunch of banshees." I agreed with him.

"Has ANYONE actually done any practise at all this week?" Then he spotted me at the back of the room. Peering through his thick spectacle lenses, he demanded "And who are you?"

I opened my mouth to answer, but Ron beat me to it. "His name is Jock Weddell, sir. He wants to play an instrument!"

Considering I was only there out of curiosity, I was not entirely pleased that Ron had dropped me in it so to speak, by deciding I was going to learn to play music. The puzzled look on Mr. Rask's face changed to a big smile. "Jock, is it?" he asked in his soft Devonshire accent. I stood up, looking a bit self-conscious as the whole band grinned at me. "Yes, sir, but my name is actually Leslie." I replied firmly.

He looked at the band and grinned. They knew what was in his mind, for he had no Bass player. He called me to the front, and taking hold of the sleeve of my school jumper, he said, "By gum you are a big lad, aren't you?" My friends all laughed, and Freddie Charlesworth said "He is a good bloke Mr. Rask, just right for you-know-what!" Again, more laughter rattled forth at my expense.

"Come with me Leslie, I've got the very thing for you!" Sheepishly, I followed him to the instrument storeroom, and on a lower rack, sat an enormous brass instrument. Mr Rask got hold of it, and pulled it free of the rack and placed it on its side on a table. "There you are Leslie - just the right size for a big fellow like you!"

I looked at it in awe, and with a mixture of excitement and wonder. For a moment or two, I could hardly contain myself, because I wanted to have a blow on it. Mr. Rask was a wise and experienced music teacher, and he read my thoughts.

"It's called the Double B flat bass. You play it like this." He picked it up and rested it awkwardly on one knee as he puffed out a few sonorous notes.

I loved it!

"Can I try, please?"

Mr. Rask said "Let's give it a good wash out first; it has been sitting unused on that rack for a couple of years now. Come back tomorrow night at band practice time, and it will be ready for you."

I was so excited all the next day, and only picked at my evening meal, which was something most unusual for me. Ron was pleased. "I told you he was a good bloke. Now he will teach you how to play the bass."

And Mr. Rask did. For the next two years I never missed a lesson or a band practice, and was soon contributing a steady 'oompah, oompah, oompah' underneath everything the rest of the band played. My rhythm was not always correct, and there were many wrong notes too, but as I got better, my usefulness increased in the band.

One day Mr. Rask took a few of us to the huge Earls Court Exhibition Centre, where the Royal Tournament, an annual spectacular showcase for the Armed Forces, was being held over three weeks.

Regiments and Bands from around the World participated in this spectacular, and we sat with our hearts beating in excitement, as we watched the show. The Royal Navy Field Gun crew were spectacular; this involved four gun crews of men pulling a cannon mounted on a four-wheeled carriage with ropes around the course set in the arena. You can see the 'last' gun run at this wonderful tournament on YouTube at the following link. Paste it onto the internet and go see it. https://youtu.be/32s4qCCFnmk.

There were obstacles to cross over, that involved disassembling the gun from the carriage, the wheels to remove, and the whole thing to be lifted and heaved over the obstacles, and reassembled, and pulled at breakneck speed down the sand and sawdust tracks in the main arena. Competition between the gun crews was fierce, and they practiced night and day, to get that speed up, and beat the records.

One year, after a visit of several hours to a local pub, two of the gun crews decided to have an unofficial race. They took two of the gun carriages down a London subway entrance, steps and all, and got them firmly stuck in the narrow aperture at the bottom of a long flight of stairs. There was hell to pay, for the London Underground was not amused, and presented the Royal Navy with a large bill for the cost of repairs to the tiling, hire of a crane to remove the gun carriages, and repairs to the beautiful Victorian style stairs. The team were severely reprimanded for their actions, and the whole incident was eventually put down to 'high spirits'!

Various attractions were on the three-week programme that year, including the RAF Parachute team who dropped down from the high roof of the Arena, and the Royal Military Police dog team doing their wonderful tricks. I particularly enjoyed that, thinking of Jed left back on the farm.

Other events came and went during the evening, and then it was time for the massed bands of the Royal Marines. The lights went low and the commentator started his build up, with a brief description of the history of the Royal Marines.

Then suddenly we heard a bugle sound from somewhere high in the gods of the building, followed by the thunderous sound of drum rolls. The lights went on full blast, and there they were - 200 splendidly dressed Royal Marines Bandsmen in their immaculate blue uniforms and white pith helmets, marching into the arena from all four corners.

It was astounding. The music was glorious and stimulating, and I could feel the thrill of it all as I gasped at the sights and sounds. I decided there and then that I was going to join the Royal Marines Band Service, and one year later on my sixteenth birthday as I mentioned in Chapter One, I was accepted, and sent as a new boy recruit to the Royal Marines School of Music in Deal, in the fair county of Kent.

Before I leave Fortesque House school behind completely, it is worth mentioning that a few years after my residency there, it was destroyed completely by fire. There were no suspicious circumstances, and the authorities suspected old electrical wiring was the cause. It was also lucky that this happened when there were no children or adults in the school, during a summer holiday break, after the headmaster and his wife had gone on holiday to France.

11. *'Demobbed, and 'Hello' to 'Civvy' Street'*

My 18 month tour of duty with the Royal Marines Band in HMS 'Terror' was almost up, when I applied for a position in the Singapore Radio Orchestra.

This came about by chance, for I was an avid listener to all big swing bands on the World service of the BBC, and the local radio stations. The Singapore Radio big band was a weekly feature and I never missed their broadcasts, and one day I decided to write a letter to the director of Music, at the Radio Station.

I told him I was a big fan of the band, and that I played the trombone in the Marine Band, and asked if it was possible to visit the Radio station and witness one of the recording sessions.

To be honest, I never really expected a reply from such a busy person, but one day I got a very nice letter from a Mr. Gus Styne, inviting me to come along on the next rehearsal, and to bring my trombone with me!

I told my Band officer, and he said to 'go for it' because opportunities like this didn't come along every day. I decided to forget the normal slow moving civilian bus service, and splurged out on a taxi ride from the Naval Base to the Radio station at Caldecott Hill, some 12 miles away, and climbed out of the cab feeling nervous, but excited and determined to play well.

Mr. Styne's secretary was waiting for me, and ushered me straight into a large auditorium that was almost freezing cold from the air conditioning system. I was dressed in light slacks and a 'T' shirt!

The band was already sitting there, having rehearsed one piece of music before making a recording, and Gus Styne was at the piano.

He turned and said 'Hello, you must be Les Weddell?" All the band members were wearing woolly cardigans, and Gus said apologetically, "Sorry, I forgot to tell you it is cold in here!"

There were five saxophones, four trumpets, and two trombones, plus drums, string bass, guitar, and of course Gus Styne, on piano.

"As you can see, we only have two trombones, and I thought it would be nice if you could join us today to make the section a little larger, as it is supposed to be four trombones, but we can't find anyone else in Singapore good enough to join the section"

The lead trombone player was a Filipino, and he was the resident trombonist with the station and a good player as well as being a nice chap, and he introduced me to the young Chinese lad playing second trombone.

Several years later, this young chap was to take over from me as the resident trombonist, when I left Singapore to return to the UK; his name was John Chew, and he was willing to learn, and asked me to give him some lessons which I happily did, free of charge.)

I enjoyed playing with the band that day, and at the end of the recording session, we all went to the staff canteen for a cold drink and a snack. The lead trombone player, Romano Cortez, asked me if I could make it every week for the recordings, and if I could, he would fix it with Gus for me to be paid.

So for the next six weeks or so, I played third trombone in the Singapore Radio big Band, and my mates in the marine band suddenly started to listen to the broadcasts. There was some jealously when I was let off duties now and then to go to the radio station, but the Band Officer would just say to those that complained, that if they did as much practice as I did, maybe they too could get some work with civilian bands.

There was nothing in service regulations stopping us from doing so, provided we were available for official duties, and I was only allowed to go in my free time for broadcasts, but never excused when on official duties with the Marine band.

Two months before I was due to end my tour of duty in Singapore, an incident happened that was to change my life. The Radio Orchestra had to play on official Singapore Government duties too, and part of these duties included performing for important occasions at the Prime Minister's official dinners and garden parties, for foreign dignitaries.

On such jobs, the Radio Orchestra personnel would be trusted to be on their best behaviour, and be ready to play whenever they were required. This could be within half an hour or perhaps an hour, after arriving. At this particular event that was to favour my future, it was a garden party for the Prime Minister, entertaining many top representatives from around the World, that had attended a big conference in Singapore, concerning economic stability in the Far East.

The orchestra was allowed to have a drink or two of alcohol supplied from the main bar, and this could be anything you fancied, from a small beer up to the finest champagne. Romano Cortez, the staff trombonist, went over the top, and got drunk.

When the time came for the orchestra to sit down ready to play, they were positioned only a few feet behind a podium of microphones. This would be where the Prime Minister of Singapore would address his guests, with the press of the World in attendance.

The venue was the former official residence of the British Governor, when Singapore was under British Administration, and had now been renamed the 'Istana Negara' (National House) by the government of the Republic of Singapore.

This was a very important event being held on a balmy night in the beautiful gardens and lawns of the Istana Negara, or Government House. Coloured lights adorned the trees and bushes, and the palm trees swayed in the gentle cooling breeze of the evening, with around five hundred guests, all seated at splendid dining tables, waiting for the Prime Minister to speak.

His speeches were legendary, and people listened to them around the World.

The Prime Minister began his speech and ten minutes or so passed by, and meanwhile, the lead trombone player was bursting to use the latrine. On this occasion, it was only the eight musicians of the staff Orchestra that were required, and were in full view of everyone at the event.

Romano Cortez asked the person next to him to pass on a message down the line to Gus Styne, that he really needed to go to the latrine immediately, as he just could not hold it in any longer. Gus was furious, and said he could not leave, but the trombone player decided he had to go. Trying to get into a crouching position so nobody would see him moving away, he caught the edge of the long wooden music stand holding the music, with his foot, and it flipped up in the air with a clatter, and all the music went flying into the air onto the lawns.

Romano fled as fast as he could move to the nearest latrine, but was not allowed back into the orchestra to play. The Prime Minister had momentary stopped in mid speech to turn around and see what was happing, and that was it for our friend the trombone player. The next day he was sacked from the Radio Orchestra, and his work Visa cancelled, and told to leave the Country. The last we heard from him was a few weeks later, when he phoned one of the members in the Orchestra, and told him he was now working in a Bangkok nightclub band.

Gus phoned me at the Marine Band office and asked if I wanted the job full time, as staff trombonist with the Singapore Radio Orchestra, and of course, I said yes, if I could get out of the Royal Marines Band Service, he said there would be no problem for me securing a work permit and a one year contract with the Singapore Government.

It was by sheer luck that just at this time, the British Armed Forces were being cut drastically in size because it was deemed such large numbers were no longer necessary for defence of the UK, and it was taking a very large chunk of the national economy to afford it all.

With the guidance of my Band Officer, I was allowed to buy my discharge, since I had served nine years of the twelve, that I had signed up for. The Admiralty charged me £75 to get out of the Marines, but sent me a cheque a few months later via the Singapore Radio Station, for the same amount, saying I should not have been charged a sum of money in the first place!

I had to satisfy the Navy that I had a 'proper job' and a contract to go with it, and they allowed me to walk out of the gates of HMS 'Terror' and the Royal Marines Band Service, for the very last time.

My stay as a civilian working in Singapore at the Radio station lasted nearly ten years. During this period, the television studios were constructed, and the new television service came into operation.

The staff band, now with a new title of the RTS orchestra, (Radio and Television Orchestra) of which I was now a permanent member, performed on TV as well as radio programmes, accompanying vocalists, and providing the music for variety shows in all the main cultures in Singapore.

I learned to speak the Malay language well enough to impress the taxi drivers, for they were not used to a Scotsman speaking in anything but 'garbled English' as one of my local friends so inaptly put it!

It soon became apparent to me that extra money could be made by arranging music for local vocalists, and the lads in the band taught me how to arrange music. This skill was to become invaluable to me later on when I returned to the UK.

There were many wonderful musical jobs that came along in my ten years in Singapore, including playing for name artists such as Shirley Bassey, Matt Monro, Tony Christie, Jane Russell, the Dutch Swing College Jazz Band and many more; but I'm too modest to mention the complete list, as you may think I'm being a big fibber. I assure you it is all true, and those are memories that will never leave me. What would have been the biggest of all never happened, because we (the RTS orchestra) were asked to play for Sammy Davis Jr on a special TV programme, but the poor man died three weeks before he was due to travel to Singapore for the event.

Accents can be deceiving dear reader, as you will most probably know, and can be misinterpreted, if one does not listen carefully. Take the first band rehearsal for the American Film star Jane Russell, for her show in the Singapore Coconut Grove Club, for example. The band sat down in front of the assembled music stands on which the music was already placed neatly in order of performance. The Musical director was Australian, and he simply raised his hands and brought down his baton for us to begin playing the first piece.

We started playing the music and it seemed to fall apart after a while, so he stopped the noise and said in a loud voice, 'Try it from section 'I'!' In rehearsals, the music director may decide to start anywhere, so we did not question his request, and started playing at letter 'I' even though we had not yet reached letter B.

He immediately shouted for us to stop again. 'I said, from letter 'I', Guys!' So we started again from the same place. Confusion reigned, for the band sounded even worse than before, and in desperation, the Aussie banged his music stand and shouted for us to stop. 'What the hell is the matter with you all? Don't any of you speak English?'

The drummer was a little quicker than the rest of us, and said loudly, 'Do you mean letter A?' The Aussie looked at us all and said 'Yes! That's what I've been trying to tell you – from letter 'I'!' There was a sigh of relief all round, and peals of laughter, and our Australian friend grinned and said 'Sorry guys, it's me that can't speak English!'

With some degree of modesty, I relate the following short story; at that time I was a tall, handsome young man, and used to comb my hair back across my head in the fashion of many Film stars of that day. Quite often I was mistaken for someone else, and you know the old saying that 'everyone has a double'?

I recall walking into an elevator in one of the posh Hotels in the city centre with two of the guys from the radio orchestra. Just as the doors began to close, two young Chinese girls shouted, so we opened the doors and they got in.

They took one look at me and started giggling, and spoke in Mandarin. My friends were slightly amused, and told me afterwards the girls thought I was 'Loger Moore'! (I.e. Roger Moore; the British actor that played the very popular 'Saint' detective television series that was currently being aired in the new Singapore Television service, and later, the role of James Bond 007) There are many other memories from those ten wonderful years I spent in Singapore, and not all of them are good.

I recall the general lack of employment amongst the local population along with the poverty too. Many destitute men and women sleeping on the streets, clothed in rags and begging for food, or pennies; thankfully, this was all about to change, for a new and dynamic group of bright people had taken over the reins of government, when Singapore became a Republic.

Today, Singapore is a fascinating city for any foreigner to explore. Besides the world-class hotels and business opportunities for companies old and new, it has a maze of exciting back streets and quarters to be explored.

From the up market classy wine bars and office café's amongst the skyscrapers of the downtown business sector around Collier Quay, to the wonderful 'Change Alley' where you can change currencies, and buy bargains from the many stalls and shops in the cosy closeness of the narrow street.

Hop on their superb Mass Transport System, and you will be rapidly whisked around the city in the clean, comfortable air- conditioned trains that Singaporeans are rightly proud of.

When I was a young man working at the Radio and Television centre, I had a good knowledge of where to go, where to eat, and the prices of most things in the shops.

One of my favourite places to visit was the Singapore Cold Storage supermarket, in Orchard Road, because they made the most delicious ice cream, and having had a good feed and cooling off in the air conditioning of the American style ice cream parlour, I could walk into the next room, and buy frozen foods to take home.

Nowadays, there are several World famous supermarkets, but the Singapore Cold Storage was the forerunner of them all, and it is still exactly on the same premises today, and just as popular with the locals as well as visitors.

Every Singaporean has a decent apartment or house in which to live, and there are hundreds of tower blocks brightly painted to fit in with the surrounding environment. A stark contrast from the days when I was there as a young man, when there were still thousands of wood shacks with corrugated tin roofing, large sections of jungle growing to the edge of the roads. Slums, in other words.

In the City itself, if you want to sample the tastiest food dishes of the World, you can find them in China town, Little India, and a little further out of the city centre there is the Malay town of Geylang.

On a recent visit to the Lion city, I found that there was very little left that I recognized from those far off days; the obvious was the central grass park called the 'Padang' in front of city hall, where the occupying Japanese army surrendered to the Commonwealth forces at the end of WW2.

I remember talking with elderly Singaporeans back in the 1960's that had lived under the Japanese occupation. They told me that you had to learn to speak basic Japanese or risk a beating.

Singapore was practically crime free after a few months of occupation, for the Japanese soldier was highly trained and obedient, and followed strict rules from his superiors, that the criminals were taken out in the street and executed on the spot in front of an assembled crowd, forced from their homes to witness the death of the culprit. There was no court appearance or let-offs. (Perhaps they should adopt some of these ideas today, in the West!)

Japanese rule was absolute. They ran the occupied territory exactly along the same lines as in their own country, and expected respect of authority from everyone. Yet many people said that if you learned to speak Japanese and showed that you were a good citizen and did not forget your manners in bowing to them, the average Japanese soldier was ok, and would often grant you access to something he was not officially supposed to do.

Today the Padang is still kept in good condition and is now surrounded by tall office blocks and hotels, and if you look closely, you will still see the cricket pavilion at the far end of the park, and behind it, the Victoria Halls sheltering in the foreground of glass faced office blocks.

The fall of Singapore was another example of bungled planning. British General Percival and his Superiors back in London, were all convinced that the Japanese invasion would come from the sea, and had placed their main defences, including huge long range guns, on the wrong side of the Island.

Winston Churchill actually warned the Generals about this, but his words fell on deaf ears, and the Japanese Army simply marched across the Johor Causeway from mainland Malaya, into a weakly defended part of Singapore Island named 'Woodlands,' and took the Island rapidly, without much resistance.

When the war officially ended, Singapore was practically intact, because there had been no heavy bombing by Japanese or Allied warplanes. The residents were soon supplied with food stocks, followed by health care, and re–organization of the British Civilian Expatriates Government administration. Within a few short years, Singapore was once again on the way back to becoming a leading business and commerce hub in the Far East.

The history of the Republic of Singapore began when it gained its independence from Britain and became a republic, following a secession from the Federation of Malaysia on 9th August 1965. After the separation, the fledgling nation had to become self-sufficient, and faced problems including mass unemployment, housing shortages, welfare and medical care, anda lack of natural resources, such as petroleum.

During Lee Kuan Yew's term as prime minister from 1959 to 1990, his administration curbed unemployment, raised the standard of living, and implemented a large-scale public housing programme. The country's economic infrastructure was developed, racial tension was mostly eliminated and an independent national defence system was created.

In 1990, Goh Chok Tong succeeded Lee Kuan Yew as Prime Minister. During his tenure, the country tackled the economic impacts of the 1997 Asian financial crisis and the 2003 SARS outbreak, as well as terrorist threats posed by the Jemaah Islamiah (JI) post-September 11 and the Bali bombings. In 2004 Lee Hsien Loong, the eldest son of Lee Kuan Yew, became the third prime minister.

12. *'There's no place like home'*

It was hard to tear myself away from Singapore, but I always knew that someday I had to return to Britain to further my career in music, and eventually buy a house and settle down. Therefore, the day finally arrived when I was at the airport with my bags ready to board a flight to the UK.

Two days before this, I had a farewell party with the members of the Radio Orchestra. It was held in the Jubilee Indian Restaurant in Jalan Sultan, known locally as the 'Arab street sector' of Singapore, where today the same restaurant still stands.

Their speciality was the tastiest curry prawns ever, and these things were giant size, not those tiny little things they pass as 'king prawns' in some stores today.

Three of those monsters filled you up, together with the saffron rice and other side dishes. Another wonderful dish is 'Daging Limbu' which is beef stewed slowly in coconut and other ingredients unknown to me, until it is so tender it practically falls apart in your mouth. This is a wonderful and tasty treat, and I recommend this to anyone who is going to travel to the orient for a holiday, or on business.

It was a sad time, for I had known these friends for ten years, and there were tears shed as we all stood up at the end of the meal to bid each other farewell. I kept in contact with them by letter for a year or two, on my return to the UK, until eventually we lost track of each other, as we all got on with our lives.

Coming back to England after 10 years abroad was quite a shock for me. In Singapore, everyone wore bright, colourful clothing, but I soon noticed that this was not so in England. In the early seventies, most young people wore dark clothes and to me, they were drab looking clothes with no distinctive style to them. This was not to last, thankfully, as it was but a fashion fad, and the age of the flair trousers for men soon came back in, along with rock 'n Roll, and women started wearing brighter, and shorter clothes, as the summer days came back.

What shocked me the most, was the existence of sex shops blatantly advertising their (to me) disgusting wares in the windows. I realized rather quickly that I'd had a sheltered life from such things in Singapore and other Far East cities, because these shops were just not existent there in the seventies.

But there were a couple of really good things I liked; especially the progress the BBC had made, for they were by this time broadcasting their television programmes in colour.

Within a few days, I had moved from London after getting nowhere fast trying to find work as a musician, and went up to Manchester, as an English friend I had met in Singapore, had told me this would be a better place to try and find work.

Phoning my friend on arrival at Gatwick Airport, he invited me to stay at his house for a week or two until I found somewhere to live, and a job. It turned out to be a wise move, for it was a few weeks before I got to know some of the local musicians by visiting pubs they played in. They all gave me the same advice; join the Musician's Union, so I did. I had left my friend's house after a week not wanting to abuse his generosity, and moved to the YMCA, because my savings were almost gone, and I was getting desperate to find work. Every day I visited the Musicians union offices to see if there was any work I could do.

This paid off when I walked in one day, and they said to contact a chap that was based in London, known as a 'fixer' in the music business. His job was to fix up the musicians for bands in seaside towns and elsewhere, that wanted a band for summer shows and theatres around the country. I was offered a summer season of 16 weeks in Torquay, a very nice town in Devon. The area is known as the 'English Riviera' because of its mild climate, most of the year.

First of all I went to the theatre, for they always have a list of accommodation available for artists to use, and I moved into a bed and breakfast guest house not far from the theatre, for two nights. However, I was lucky to find a Caravan for summer rental, in a proper caravan park, that had a mains electricity supply, and a small shop.

Not ever having any experience of such a vehicle, I did not have a clue about how to use it properly, and the first two nights I slept on the narrow seats.

I got talking to the folks that occupied the caravan parked next to mine, and they came into my caravan and demonstrated how the seats and the table could be arranged to make a double bed, as well as how to use the cooker. This required the use of a butane gas bottle, and the one that was stowed in the outside locker, was empty. That was soon rectified, for everything I needed was right there on the

Caravan site in the shop, including butane gas, and a small range of foods that were to say the least, expensive.

I soon found out that a large supermarket was located a mile down the road, and the times of the buses passing it and our caravan site, and there were no more uncomfortable nights going to sleep with no food, trying to sleep on narrow seats!

The job in the theatre was excellent. I enjoyed working there with such good musicians, but sadly the season was soon over and meant I had to leave the caravan and go elsewhere to find a place to live, as well as a another job. In the off season or autumn, a seaside town is almost closed up for musical jobs, so the only thing for it was to go back to Manchester, for at least I knew a few musician contacts there as well as the staff in the office of the Musician's Union.

Living in a comfortable rented 'bedsitter' apartment this time, I found it to be luxury after the Caravan, even though I had enjoyed my stay in it.

The landlady was very nice, and helped me with tips about places around the City that I might try to find musical work. After a few weeks of not finding any job at all, I decided I really had to make a decision about my future.

I got a break when I phoned the union office one morning and they told me the 'fixer' that booked me for the Torquay show had been trying to get in touch with me.

Telephoning the number they gave me, the agent or Fixer' as musicians named them, told me he had received good reports from the Musical Director of the Torquay summer show, and he offered me a six week tour with the 'Comedians', a group of Britain's top funny men, and of course I jumped at it. It was a pick-up band, which means people selected from anywhere in the UK that the 'Fixer' had on his books. The line-up was one trumpet, one trombone, two saxophones (alto and tenor) and piano, bass, and drums, plus an MD or Musical Director, who usually was the pianist.

I said goodbye to my landlady, and took an express bus to Peterborough, the venue of our first 'gig,' or show. No bother finding 'digs,' and the show ran for a week, with much success, before the whole show moved onto to the next town. I made good money in the six weeks the tour lasted, and one of the musician's in the band told me to go to Southport, in Lancashire, for he said it was not far from Liverpool and Manchester, and there was also a large holiday camp nearby.

In the music game when you are just getting started, you have to take every scrap of information and advice and act on it, for there is no second chance. I decided there was nothing wrong with trying this idea, and moved to Ainsdale, a small village (at that time) near Southport. I decided that I needed to find a day job, and was lucky to get a job in a factory, making confectionery for big name stores, but my luck was not to last, for the company went broke, and closed.

I kept in touch with the local Musician's Union offices in Manchester as well as the Liverpool branch, too, and it eventually paid off again, because I was getting known as a trombonist, and work on the weekends started trickling in. I also started teaching at that time, and accepted a position teaching children to play brass instruments in three schools, at the request of the Merseyside educational music service. At this time, I still had not learned to drive a car.

So, I had to take a train from Ainsdale into Liverpool; catch a bus that went through the Mersey Tunnel to Birkenhead, and then another bus that took me to the first of my three schools, all roughly in the same area. It took me ages to get to each school, but they scheduled the music lessons to accommodate my travel arrangements.

Then summer came around again and I was offered a contract for sixteen weeks in the Pontins holiday camp nearby, in Ainsdale, which turned out to be a good one with a very good band, and brought more contact with other musicians, and eventually led to more weekend work in the theatres in Liverpool, as well as nightclubs in Manchester.

Sticking with the day job of teaching in schools, I decided it was still not enough, and when I was asked to go on a cruise liner for five months with the band out of the holiday camp, I foolishly agreed.

By this time, I had met, and married my wife. She started work in a department store in Southport town centre, and said I should go on the cruise, as it meant more income for us. So off I flew with the rest of the band to San Juan, in Porto Rico, where the cruise ship 'Adventurer' was alongside the jetty. I hated it. I was away from my new wife, and was miserable as hell, spending a fortune on long distance phone calls lasting up to half an hour talking to her, calling at least twice a week.

She was lonely. This made me feel even worse, for I realized I had put work before her, and made a terrible decision to take the ship job. After five long months we returned to the UK, and I vowed never ever, to leave her again for such a long time.

As I was away for five months, it meant that my connections with local musicians had faded somewhat, so I had to build my contacts up again. It was during a pantomime season at the Empire theatre in Liverpool, that I met some of the musician's that travelled every day from Blackpool. They told me I was wasting my time living in Southport, and should move to Blackpool, because that was where the work was all year around. They were right.

Contacting the Music office at the Blackpool Tower Company, as it was known then, I was given a one night gig in the Empress Ballroom, as a trial. I will always remember that day, for my wife came with me to see Blackpool, for it was a first time visit to the resort for us both. We made sure we checked into a bed and breakfast house, then spent the rest of the morning exploring the 'Golden Mile' of the seafront.

We went on the big dipper at the Pleasure beach; had ice cream, fish and chips, and finally returned to the bed and breakfast house in time for me to change into my 'evening dress,' that was worn by all musicians on casual engagements.

I got my wife into the Ballroom without any problems, and she went to sit down upstairs in the balcony, whilst I went to the stage side and found the Band Leader. It was a wonderful evening of playing super music for experienced dancers that showed their appreciation of the fine music being played, with applause at the end of every tune.

The next day, the office called me at the bed and breakfast guest house, and asked if I would like to go in the Tower Circus band, as they needed a trombone player, and it was a five month long season.

So began my first long term job in the circus, and at this point, I think I should give a short history lesson on the Blackpool Tower Complex, as the Circus is built right underneath the main support girders.

This is only short, I promise!

The idea for building the tower came about when Blackpool Mayor John Bickerstaffe commissioned the design of a new landmark for the town, after he visited the Great Paris Exhibition in 1889, and was impressed by the Eiffel Tower.

When he returned to Blackpool, he set up a committee of businessmen in order to raise the funds to build a similar design in the town. In 1891, he invested £2,000 of his own money to form, with other local investors, the *Blackpool Tower Company Limited*. The company was registered on 19 February 1891.

Two Lancashire architects, James Maxwell and Charles Tuke, designed the Tower and oversaw the laying of its foundation stone on 29th of September 1891, when a time capsule was buried beneath it. When the Tower finally opened on 14 May, 1894, both men had died. The total cost for the design and construction of the tower and buildings was about £290,000.

Five million bricks, 2,500 tonnes of iron and 93 tonnes of cast steel were used to construct the tower. The cast steel and iron are distributed in such a way that if it did ever collapse it would fall into the sea. The tower buildings occupy a total of 5,050 sq meters (6,040 sq yards) Unlike the Eiffel Tower, Blackpool Tower is not quite free-standing, because its base is hidden by the building, which houses the Tower Circus.

Almost from the moment they completed it Blackpool became a favourite playground for millions of people taking their annual factory, or works, holidays. They came from all over Britain, and especially from the surrounding towns and cities in the North West of England.

Many thousands of these day-trippers and holidaymakers led dreary lives, working in low paid jobs in the cotton mills and manufacturing companies in the hundreds of little hamlets and towns in Lancashire and Cheshire, and a break in Blackpool was a treat for them to really look forward to when holidays were given by their employers.

Apart from the Tower complex, there are also the famous piers; North, Central and South, and they have attractions and seasonal shows to attract the visitors. Take a walk up the so called 'Golden Mile' and you will come to the World famous Blackpool Pleasure beach, a paradise for thrill seekers young and old, on the rides and attractions. At night, it is like fairyland, when all the coloured lights are switched on.

We moved from Ainsdale to Blackpool, and found another comfortable apartment, this time with four bedrooms. We did not need them all, but we took the apartment because the rent was very reasonable. We lived there for five years until we had saved enough money to buy our first house. My wife found a day job in a restaurant kitchen, and I was working every night in the Winter Gardens playing for dances, and we began to save some much needed money.

There was enough musical work to keep me going throughout the week, because in those heady days of the seventies and eighties, there was public dancing in the ballrooms, and large corporate dinners almost every night, besides other gigs offered by working bands in clubs and other venues around the area. It was not long before we had our first child, and so my wife had to stop work.

This was a happy era for both of us, as our family had grown to five with the birth of our third child, and in the mid Eighties we decided it was time to move away from Blackpool, and bought a house in Preston, where we still live today.

As we progressed into the nineties, it was apparent the work with bands and being a musician on a regular basis, was coming to an end.

I decided to take up teaching brass instruments. I secured employment teaching several hours daily, in several local independent schools (fee paying) in the Fylde and the surrounding district, and eventually was asked by the Lancashire Music Service to join their ranks.

This was ideal, for that allowed me to take weekend musical work playing with bands on one night jobs, and I was now enjoying more time with my kids, and especially in the school holidays.

We purchased a large caravan and towed that around the UK for three or four years. When we finally sold it, we decided to go further afield and booked holidays in France, driving to the campsite, where we had a fully furnished and comfortable static caravan, that is it was set in concrete, so it could not be towed away.

When our children grew into their late teens we could trust them to look after themselves as well as the house, and it presented my wife and I with the opportunity to travel to far away places such as Singapore, Thailand, Australia and New Zealand, Florida, and other wonderful places.

Having arranged 25 special arrangements for 21 trombones and 3 saxes plus four trumpets and a full Latin rhythm section, I advertised in on a Web site and got an email from a Professor of Dentistry who lived in America, and as she and her husband were both trombonists, she wondered if I would be interested in bringing the music over and playing it with some of her friends?

Prior to this offer I had been invited by the Wigan jazz Club to give a special concert with the trombones at Wigan Pier Concert Room. This was ideal, for it gave us a chance to 'iron out' any mistakes in the copying or arranging ideas. We need not have worried, for it sounded wonderful.

So the trip was on to Philadelphia, which I found to be a very nice city with friendly people; it is also famous for its long association with jazz music, and my hosts fixed up a musical session at the Bucks County campus of the University, I was pleasantly surprised because 30 trombone players had turned up, and six saxes, and six trumpet players too! It seemed everyone wanted to get in on the opportunity to play with a unique band. The sound was absolutely superb.

My good friends had assembled the best trombonists they could find, and it was a most gratifying experience for me to hear my arrangements being played. There were several (now retired) side men that had played back in the heydays of the big bands, with Count Basie, Duke Ellington and Woody Herman, as well as a mix of eager young players, to bring the best out of those musical arrangements.

I was in awe of these retired musicians, for they had been members of three of the most famous Big Bands in jazz in the World. And here was I, an unknown nobody from the UK in the same room, and playing music with them!

We had time for only a short rehearsal before we played the concert, and although it was recorded, the results were not good enough for commercial distribution. With financial backing, another two or three rehearsals would certainly have brought each piece up to scratch, as well as provide the opportunity for a proper set up for the recording engineer. But the experience was well worth the effort, and our little audience of friends and fellow musicians enjoyed it as much as we did in the band.

The idea of so many trombones is not new as it has been done before with as many as 300 or more, playing in a mass 'blow,' and is still popular today around the world in the trombone fraternity. There is a strong following of trombone players in the Netherlands, and they even have specially made small trombones manufactured for children from the age of seven years onwards. They love massed trombone performances, and you can see several such casual performances on YouTube.

Since we were only in Philadelphia for three days, our guests made it a jam packed schedule for us, and we managed to get a trip up to New York in the afternoon, and take the ferry around the bay and up the river under Brooklyn Bridge, and past the famous New York Yankees Baseball stadium.

Our trip was in February, only a few months after the dreadful destruction of the twin towers in New York, and as the ferry passed the banks of buildings on Manhattan Island, we saw the huge gaping hole where the towers had once stood, and it was a poignant moment of sadness for everyone on that vessel.

We visited a special establishment in the City of Philadelphia, which both our hosts thought would be a treat, for it was a drive in café exactly as it would have looked back in the 1940's.

Lots of coloured neon lights, chrome edged tables, a really snazzy looking juke box playing rock and roll records, and of course all the waitresses were dressed in short skirts and 'flying' around the place on roller skates!

We ordered grilled cheese sandwiches and a proper Milkshake. It was a most enjoyable half hour of nostalgia, sitting in that café watching those girls scoot around with trays full of shakes and burgers and fries (chips!).

I am indebted to our guests Dr. Leslie Kilgren and her partner Joe for their wonderful hospitality, and efforts in bringing it all together.

My wife and I have been back to visit America, to the sunshine state of Florida; and of course we took in the Walt Disney Parks, but our main reason for the visit was to see the Kennedy Space Station.

We booked a tour that would include lunch with a former astronaut and to witness the launch of the Space shuttle 'Atlantis.' We had the lunch, but there were some red faces amongst the organizers when it was discovered there were no astronauts available for the tour, or to take lunch with. To make up for the shortcoming, they gave us a free tour of a new exhibition, which was a mock-up of the ISS, or

International Space Station. It was the same size as the real one up in orbit right now, and we were surprised that it was so big.

The day before our visit to the Kennedy Space Centre, a thunderstorm hit the area, and lightening hit the launch tower, and to be on the safe side until they had thoroughly inspected everything, the launch was postponed.

It went successfully two days later, but by this time we were back home in Britain and watched it on TV. It is a wonderful place to visit, and really, you need to be there early in the morning to spend a complete day to view all the features.

We also went to the 'Magic Kingdom' in Orlando and spent a wonderful few days touring the other attractions as well. The Walt Disney Magic Kingdom was wonderful! Just watching the looks on the faces of little children was rewarding in itself and the only regrets we had was that we could not afford to take our own children there when they were little.

One thing we found useful to pass on is this; if you ever want to go visit Disneyland, then do yourself a favour and stay either with them in a Disney on site hotel, or at the Hard Rock Café or other Hotels in Universal Studios. That is a wonderful place for adults and children, and certainly is worth the effort and the extra cost. Staying elsewhere (as we did, in an Inn) can be in a remote area with no bus service, as we found out. But at Disneyland they have a monorail that travels around all their properties and attractions, stopping at all their hotels en route.

You really are better off buying an all in day ticket via your holiday travel agent, or look at the offers some major airlines offer, from time to time with discounts.

Universal studios are nothing short of fabulous! If you don't have kids this is ideal for you too, and if you do have kids still go! They have a large section there dedicated to all the famous Cartoon characters, and it is a delight to walk down this special street full of characters. You can look up at a building and suddenly there is 'Spiderman' climbing up a wall, or 'Daffy Duck' comes out of a door and is being chased by Bugs Bunny, all done with holograms and other clever techniques.

Classic cars, the original full size steam engine used in 'Back to the Future' movies, and of course, the massive 'Jaws' shark hangs on a special display rigging for all to have their photo taken, as I did, with my head inside his jaws.

Take a trip on a boat on a lake and suddenly a huge (plastic) crocodile jumps up out the water towards the side of the boat. This is not recommended if you are elderly, or faint of heart! Walk down 'Gangster Alley' and watch the cops shooting it out with the bad guys, as a genuine Dixie band plays some cool jazz on the corner of the street. Have a beer in a genuine western saloon bar, served by a barman with a large handlebar moustache, and wearing a large white apron, packing a six shooter too.

Come nightfall and the whole place turns into magic land.

Loads of pubs of all kinds and cocktail bars and dining rooms, Cabaret shows, are all there for the taking. There is no way anyone can be bored taking a holiday of a lifetime at Universal Studios in Orlando, Florida.

In the 'Hard Rock Café' we had a drink at the main bar, over which is suspended an open top full sized pink Cadillac limousine on a mahogany wooden shelf, or plinth. You can find out details of taking a holiday in the resort by going online and checking vacation deals.

We also enjoyed a whole day in the Disney Epcot centre, which is a real treat for all the family. Unfortunately, it was the rainy season at the time of our visit and we got soaked several times during the day with downpours. However, there are plenty of attractions and places to shelter from the elements, and you are never going to be bored in that wonderful place of entertainment.

13. *'Musicians are people too!'*

I cannot end this story without revealing to you some of the funny things that happen on a bandstand. The musician has the best seat in the house, when the band is on stage because he/she can see everyone, and what they are doing.

Women looking very elegant and dressed to kill for the big dinner dance, then an hour or so later, after drinking a little too much 'hooch,' they tend to let their guard down, falling on the dance floor, or off their seat at the dining table. And you would not believe the number of men coming out of the bathroom with their trouser flies open.

Requests come all the time to the Bandleader; *'Can you let my wife sing with your band?'* And a never ending question was, *'How do you become a musician?'* or my favourite, *'How do you know what to do with that slide thing on your trombone?'*

And probably the biggest insult of all, *'Do you get paid to do this?'*

M.C.'s (Master of Ceremonies) and Bandleaders can make announcements that can sound funny too...

"One gold lady's watch, and a gentleman's brief's case handed in. They are on the table by the Ladies toilet."

Then there is the tipsy guy that comes up on the stage, tripping over the flower boxes as he goes, trying to grab the microphone, and gets upset when the house security or the band leader intervene and ask him to get off the stage.

Another type that likes to find their moment of glory, is the drunk woman, or man, that manages to find how to get onto stage from the wings, and looks at the Bandleader with bleary eyes and says in a slurred voice, *'I just want to sing with the band!'*

When it comes to clothes, the normal 'standard' dress for musicians to wear at dances is evening wear; this is the standard black dinner jacket and trousers, plus a white shirt and black bow tie, and of course, black shiny dress shoes.

But some bandleaders insist on their band members wearing a uniform, sitting behind fancy music stands which have the name of the bandleader on the front. These uniforms can be just a simple T shirt, all the way up, to a specially designed band suit and shirt provided by the Bandleader or Television company.

I recall a Band I played in for sixteen weeks, in which we all had to wear a Band Blazer, which looked a bit like a Boys School jacket gone wrong. You know the type? An off colour cream stripe running around the edges of the jacket and pockets, and the Band Leader's initials on the lapels or breast pocket. Well, back in those days, I used to smoke a pipe. One night, I was wearing it to walk from my chalet to the ballroom, and it was windy, so I took the pipe out of my mouth, which I had lit in the chalet, and put it in my pocket.

Unfortunately, unknown to me, it was still 'alive' and the burning tobacco had burnt a hole in the inside covering of the jacket, and I only saved the rest of the coat by smelling it in time, to remove the contents of the pocket. It was very lucky for me that the Bandleader did not smell the burning or see any singe marks, and the next day I bought some lining material and repaired the hole in the inside pocket. At the end of the season, I simply handed the coat back to the Leader without explanation, and that was the end of it. It was barely recognizable that any damage had been done because my repair was good, and the material matched the colour of the original lining of the jacket.

In the hey days of travelling bands, they used a band bus; usually hired, but it was not unknown for a Bandleader to own his own bus and pay someone to drive and maintain the vehicle, and indeed, many famous American bands toured their country using such a mode of transport, to keep costs down.

There is the famous story told by American musicians about the great Buddy Rich band. Having completed a concert, they were on the band bus on the long way back to home, and someone switched on a portable recorder and taped the whole 'in-yer-face' scolding Buddy was ranting at the band, as he was not in the least pleased with their performance that evening.

In the Northern Dance Orchestra, we had to be smart on stage, and you needed to be careful with the band coat when you had a drink or ate a snack, not to make a mess. One young trumpet player did just this while horsing around with another musician in the band room, holding a cup of hot drinking chocolate. It went all over the front of his white shirt, and no amount of scrubbing the offending stain in the hand basin, could remove it, so he had to go on stage wearing a wet shirt. As he was sitting in the back row of the band, I don't think the public noticed it, but I bet his wife did when he got home.

Musicians and their excuses could fill volumes! I've had a few of my own when I was younger, and sometimes late getting back on stage, but just sitting down and grabbing my trombone before the music started to play.

One musician I knew was always well dressed, but sometimes would forget to put on his black dress shoes in the car, or the band room, and would turn up on stage still wearing brown shoes, or even trainers! He would realize this after a while, especially if the other guys around him were laughing, and try to hide his feet behind the narrow bandstand, so that the leader would not see his 'wrong' shoes.

Another time, on a sixteen week long summer show in the Blackpool Opera House, I recall the baritone saxophone player sitting in the saxophone section trying to get some low notes out of his instrument, without much success. He suddenly put his hand down the bell of the instrument and pulled out a bottle of whisky. He used to leave the baritone in the orchestra pit every night, as nobody in those days would touch the instruments.

Then there was the forgetful trombonist. No names, but it is true, I promise you. He finished a concert gig in Southport Theatre, and went to his car, opening the boot (trunk) to put his instrument inside.

However, he put it down on the road, as he started to talk to another band member who had parked his car in front of him, and when they finally wished each other Goodnight, he had got in his car and drove off, leaving his trombone beside the kerb!

Lucky for him that one of the door security men spotted it, and took the instrument inside the Hall to the offices, and it was the next day before our friend who will remain nameless, realized his trombone was missing! (No, it was not me!) After sitting down and going over his moves after leaving the hall, he decided to phone them, and was more than relieved to find his trombone was with them.

Another friend of mine reversed over his saxophone, which he had placed on the ground to open the boot of his car, and completely forgot about it when answering his mobile phone, and putting the car in reverse gear to get out of the parking space, ended the life of that noble instrument. Thankfully, he was insured, and the cost of a new saxophone was covered by his policy.

The most outrageous incident I remember was about a trumpet player who was lucky enough to be part of a family that was fairly rich. He had a good day job and being a non smoker and teetotal, he saved up and bought himself a Porshe sports car.

We were playing a pantomime at the Empire Theatre in Liverpool, and on the second night of the show, this chap parked his new car in an alley close to the stage door. When he came out of the orchestra pit, the stage manager suggested that he go and look at his car outside, as something had happened to it.

The car had been completely turned upside down! It was as if it was a turtle that had somehow lost its balance. The strange thing is nobody saw it, and yet it was parked close to the theatre stage door. The end result was, that this lucky fellow got a completely new car in exchange for his car, as it was almost a wreck.

Then there was the story of the famous Bandleader who used to stroll around the stage in front of the band as it was playing, and one night during a Concert to a full house in the Royal Albert Hall in London, he was moving backwards across the stage as he waved his hand up and down conducting the band, to suddenly disappear off the edge of the platform and down amongst the sound equipment cables on the floor!

Another Bandleader was doing a recording session at the famous strawberry studios, and having to fill in the details of the music the band was recording on the Performing Rights Society returns, he asked the pianist 'who was the composer of that Chopin waltz'! To explain, the pianist had arranged the tune for the band, and simply given it the title 'Chopin Waltz'.

Musicians may play like Angels at times, but I assure you they are not in that category on the bandstand. For much goes on that the public never suspect is happening. In Blackpool, back in the 1970's, there were four major dance festivals every year, starting with the Easter Junior Dance Festival, which was a week long and was over the Easter holiday break.

Then the May Dance Festival, which was the most prestigious dance festival, attracting competitors from around the World, and a bumper load of talent with lots of formation teams dancing in competitions.

This was open to all ballroom dances including the quickstep, waltz, foxtrot, tango, samba, cha-cha, Latin, and including rock and roll. That was followed by the Sequence Dance Festival in October, plus the British Open Dance Festival in November.

The Empress Ballroom orchestra supplied the music for all of these festivals, and was respected by the dancers. Over the years, various Bandleaders fronted the orchestra, and they all did a first class job. It is not easy starting a band off in the correct tempo for each dance, for there will always be opinions as to the correct tempo. That was usually addressed by the experience of the Bandleader, and when needed, the use of a metronome and an official of the British Dance Association.

These festivals are marathon sessions, and often the band, or essential kingpin players, were required to attend rehearsals of the formation teams and cabaret artist dancing exhibitions, in the morning at 11am, and have it all sorted and dusted, by 1pm.

Then we would be required to return dressed in evening suits to play from 5pm until 1 am or 2am, the next morning, with breaks every hour and a half of 25 minutes.

On week long dance festivals when you are required to play long hours, rest breaks are short, and this is the time to visit the pub and have a pint of beer, and later, consume endless supplies of chilled sandwiches brought to the band room during the evening playing sessions.

All this stuff does nothing to improve your digestive system, and consequently a large build up of gas is going to finally want to escape (if you get my meaning) and this seemed to turn into a contest in the band, as to who could produce the loudest noise, not to mention the dreadful smell!

And this usually happened when the whole band was actually playing, and trying to breathe away from that lot was impossible. Many a night the bandstand was worse than a men's room that has not been cleaned in days; the Band leader would say a few cross words to no avail, for it still continued, since the culprit or culprits, were certainly not going to own up.

In the nineteen seventies and eighties, work was plentiful for musicians in the right place at the right time, and big bands were still very popular with older audiences. Gigs in London, Glasgow, Aberdeen, and many other cities, plus on the Continent, were some of the venues the bands I played with, visited.

I had the honour of playing with some great name bands such as the Northern Dance Orchestra, the new Glenn Miller orchestra, Eric Delaney, the new Geraldo orchestra, Andy Prior Band, Empress Ballroom Orchestra, and in 'pick-up' bands to accompany name artists on one night T.V. Shows, or theatre appearances.

Each band has its own stories to tell, and there are some that are just unbelievable.

Even theatres have a tale to tell; one being the back stage of the Floral Hall in Southport.

Many famous bands and orchestras appeared there, including Stan Kenton, Blood, Sweat & Tears, Woody Herman, Ted Heath and many more.

On the building wall behind the stage to the side, musicians in visiting American bands had signed their names, and some artistic person had made a very good cartoon on the wall of a plane flying over water, and a parachute descending with a huge balloon with the words 'Doo-Wah' written in it!

It was a reference to the great Glenn Miller, who tragedy disappeared in a plane over the English Channel. Not malicious in any way, and done with a sense of humour, for all the bands that played in that beautiful hall would have played some of Glenn Millers' music.

This is a reference to the brass players using a special mute with the hand moving in and out of the instrument bell to produce a sound of 'Doo-Wah'! Trombones especially had this recurring phrase in several of Miller arrangements.

Unfortunately, the whole cartoon was painted over by the Stage staff on the instructions of the Theatre and Ballroom owners, before anyone could photograph it. Peasants-they know not what they do! For musicians, that was a bit like painting over the Mona Lisa.

There is a story concerning one band of note that had a Continental booking in Brussels, and the majority of the band travelled in a hired coach, and the Bandleader and his son followed behind in a rented transit van with all the Band gear, such as bandstands, microphones, lighting, music library, and drum kits.

As they approached Dover for the ferry, the bandleader's Son suddenly asked his Dad if all the music was packed in the van. The Bandleader decided to pull into a service station, and on checking, found to his horror that two of the specially designed trunks were missing. Between them, Father and Son had somehow forgotten to check all the boxes were loaded.

Without the music, the band would be practically useless, for the engagement was a Concert, and they must have the full complement of specially arranged music which was unique to the orchestra.

The engagement was the following evening at 7.30pm. So a plan was agreed upon.

The Father would proceed with the van behind the coach onto the ferry, and continue on the journey to Brussels, and the Son took an express train from Dover to London and up to Blackpool, where he got the two missing cases of music and loaded them into a taxi, and went to Blackpool airport and caught a domestic flight to Heathrow and another flight to Brussels, the whole affair costing the Bandleader a considerable amount of money.

It was by sheer luck that the Son managed to get the connecting flights, and he made it by taxi from the airport in Brussels, to the venue where the Concert was to be held, arriving just 30 minutes before the show was to begin.

Being a Bandleader is not all glamour, for sometimes you win some, and sometimes you lose some, when it comes to making any profit from playing music.

You have to fork out the initial investment to buy the music, have the bandstands made, provide the sound system for your band and vocalists, and the band uniforms too, if you wish them to wear such attire.

There are extra costs in paying an agent to obtain engagements for your band, and publicity too, and making a few recordings of C.D.'s helps, if you want to build up your reputation. These are usually sold at the door on entry, and given free to radio stations to play, in the town/city your band is booked to perform.

If you do not provide a bus for transport of your musicians and their equipment, you will certainly need to be prepared to pay their travel expenses, as according to expected rates set by the Musician's Union.

And of course, don't forget you will need insurance for your business, for running a band for profit making is most definitely a business. If someone falls over and hurts themselves on your bus or bandstand, you could be sued, so insurance is a must.

Most of the Leaders I worked for were decent guys, and paid us all on the evening after the job was finished, or, by cheque sent within a week, that took another five days to clear.

There are countless stories from musicians that have been cheated by Leaders in one way or another; either by design, or because they did not quite do their arithmetic correctly, and account for extras such as fuel expenses and mishaps.

I recall one chap I worked for who was a famous Bandleader, but I will not reveal his name as he is no longer with us, who arrived at the venue in Scarborough, to discover he had left his dress shoes at home, and went driving around the town centre at 5.30pm trying to find a shoe shop that was still open, finally spotting the lights still on in a small shop, and the assistant locking the door.

To her surprise, this lunatic man was hammering on the door demanding she open it again! In fear, she called the Manager, and it was only by sheer luck that the gentleman recognized the Bandleader, and opened the door to find out what the panic was about.

Not only was our intrepid Leader lucky to get a pair of dress shoes his size, but he got them at a sale price too, when he told the Shop Manager to come to the dance that evening as his guest.

Top musicians are not always treated as professionals by the general public, simply because they have no knowledge of the training, the talent required, and the hard slog to gain experience and become master of your craft. These are the men and women who supply all the wonderful music in the background on your favourite radio and television shows, the great arrangements and songs for famous singers, and who do the work in recording studios, referred to as session musicians.

Over the course of fifty years I worked with great musicians and good guys around the World, that could perform to the very top of their profession; and it was a delight to sit next to them playing the very best musical arrangements available.

I found that most of the top professionals did not drink alcohol on the gig, and that certainly stood them apart from the others that did, for their performance on solos was always impeccable.

Only a musician can experience the thrill and satisfaction of playing music to such a high standard, and the nearest I can come to explaining that feeling to you, is, to liken you to being a golfer and getting to play 18 holes with Tiger Woods.

Exhilarating, and doing something really special, you never forget for the rest of your life.

I have omitted names not to offend any of my former musical colleagues, but I assure you all the stories that concern musicians listed above, are true.

Alas, dear reader, it is time for our little journey into the past to end. As the good Sergeant Crowther would have said '*Do ye unerstan*?'

(© Copyright 2015 by Leslie J. Weddell)

'International Super Cop Harry Thompson is assigned to the vibrant city of Singapore, and can't believe his luck. That soon changes, when he finds himself number one on the hit list of the most notorious Crime Cartel in the Orient.'

My new Action-Adventure thriller, set in the Far East.

Having lived in Singapore for so many years, it was a natural choice of location in which to set my plot for my first action Novel. It is now available on Amazon Books as an e-book publication. http://amzn.com/B01M67HA04

Save the Children

http://www.savethechildren.org

A personal message from Leslie J. Weddell

Please consider joining me in supporting the SAVE THE CHILDREN fund. A non-profit organization that does superb work to help the children of the World.
They work quietly and without fanfare, and rely entirely on donations, the bulk coming from the public around the World, and from a small number of wealthy Philanthropists.

They spend 95% of the donations on saving children from starvation, providing emergency relief with follow-up long term care after tsunami, earthquake and war. They finance schemes for building water wells, schools and hospitals, providing farm equipment for self dependency, and helping to place children in proper homes. They also fund rescues of kids living on the streets in South America, India, Africa, as well as helping poor children in the USA and the UK and other parts of Europe.

Right now in 2015 thousands of children in Syria and over crowded refugee camp on the borders are in need of urgent help.

Food, clothes, medicine, tender loving care for those (and there are many of them) children in trauma at loosing their Parents.

Some of these poor kids are only two or three years old. It is easy to write about these kids, but to see them in real life is enough to make you weep.

Please give what you can afford to Save the Children to help them all.

Just £5 GBP or $10 US a month can make a huge difference. When thousands of people around the world give generously, it truly makes a huge difference to sustain the wonderful work of rescue that the Save the Children Organisation is passionately dedicated to doing.

All Children are beautiful, innocent, and the future of the human race on this Planet. No matter what colour of their skin, or language they may speak.

The Save the Children motto is; 'No Child is born to die'

I whole heartedly agree with them.

Children *are* life.

Printed in Great Britain
by Amazon